I. Introduction and Overview of Research Objectives

Labeling rules promulgated by the Food and Drug Administration ("FDA") currently prohibit many potentially useful claims concerning the heart-health benefits of replacing products such as butter or margarine with alternative fats and oils that are lower in saturated fat and/or trans fatty acids. These labeling restrictions also appear to have discouraged similar claims in advertising. The primary basis for FDA's restrictions on heart-health claims for fats and oils is that these products are high in total fat and calories, which can lead to weight gain and associated heart problems if consumers add these foods to their diet indiscriminately.

The research reported in this working paper was undertaken to determine whether health claims in print advertising can be crafted to communicate the heart benefits of *substituting* certain fats and oils for less healthy alternatives without misleading consumers into thinking that the products pose no other health risks if eaten without regard to their high caloric content. In answering this question, the following related issues are explored:

• *Do health claims cast a "halo" over a product's perceived healthiness?* Although heart- health claims for many high-fat products are currently prohibited in labeling, simple statements of nutrient content, such as "low in saturated fat" are allowed for conforming products. Within a deception framework, it would be difficult to justify more restrictive regulation of health claims unless the additional health information distorted consumer perceptions of the overall healthiness of the advertised product. For the fats and oils group, the specific concern would be that promoting a product's heart healthiness could lead a substantial number of consumers to underestimate the amount of total fat and calories in the product. Consumers also might conclude incorrectly that, irrespective of caloric content, the advertised product acted in pharmaceutical fashion to improve heart health even when added to an existing diet. Accordingly, our research included test ads with only nutrient content information, and ads that combined this information with an explicit heart-health claim. Questions were crafted to determine whether the health claim changed consumer perceptions of caloric content and, more generally, the heart healthiness of adding the test products to the diet.[2]

• *Do "substitution claims" reduce any such halo effect?* The heart-health benefits of a fat or oil might be presented in either an absolute or comparative context. An absolute claim would

---

[2] A very similar issue was explored in Murphy, D., *et al.,* "Generic Copy Test of Food Health Claims in Advertising," Bureau of Economics Staff Report, Federal Trade Commission, November 1998: 19-28. That study tested various ad treatments for a fictitious sliced cheese product that was high in calcium, but also high in saturated fat. These treatments included a simple nutrient content calcium claim and an explicit calcium-osteoporosis health claim. Consumer perceptions of the product's saturated fat content did not differ significantly between the nutrient content and health claim treatments. Due to problems in the wording of the question, however, response rates were low in all the test cells, which greatly reduced the power of the test to detect any halo effect that might have existed. As explained on p. 25 *infra,* the present study adopted wording that avoided this problem.

state simply that use of the product can help reduce the risk of heart disease. In contrast, an advertiser might specify more explicitly the dietary substitutions needed to achieve this benefit, *e.g.* "Our cooking oil is low in saturated fat. Using our oil instead of butter in cooking can help reduce your risk of heart disease." Both types of claims were tested to determine whether placing the claim in the context of a dietary substitution would avoid or reduce any inference that the advertised food can be added to an existing diet with no adverse heart-health risk.

● *If additional disclosures are needed, which are most effective?* Assuming that heart-health claims, irrespective of context, do distort consumer perceptions of a product's nutrient profile, the relevant issue is whether a disclosure or disclaimer can correct these misperceptions. Our consumer research tested the effectiveness of disclosing the product's caloric content and, alternatively, its total fat content.

II. Background

The link between diets high in saturated fat, elevated serum cholesterol levels, and heart disease is among the most firmly established diet-disease relationships in the medical literature. Empirical evidence showing a strong correlation between consumption of saturated fat and serum cholesterol levels dates back to 1957 with the pioneering work of Keys, Anderson, and Grande.[3] A substantial body of clinical evidence on the heart-health benefits of substituting monounsaturated and polyunsaturated fats for saturated fats has accumulated since then,[4] and population studies consistently have shown lower death rates from heart disease in countries that have experienced declines in saturated fat consumption.[5]

Growing evidence also has established a strong link between dietary intake of trans fatty acids (commonly found in partially hydrogenated vegetable oils) and serum cholesterol levels. This evidence has strengthened to the point where FDA now considers there to be "...a direct,

---

[3]   Keys, A., J. T. Anderson, and F. Grande, "Prediction of serum cholesterol responses of man to changes in fats in the diet," 2 *Lancet*, 1957: 959-966.

[4]   Huxley, R., S. Lewington, and R. Clarke, "Cholesterol, coronary heart disease and stroke: a review of published evidence from observational studies and randomized controlled clinical trials," 2(3) *Semin Vasc Med*, 2002, Aug: 315-23.

[5]   Most recently, a study published in the *British Medical Journal* reported that death rates from heart disease in Poland dropped by over one-third by 2002 after the Polish government lowered subsidies for saturated fats in 1991, and consumption patterns shifted from increasingly expensive saturated fats to polyunsaturated fats. *See* Witold, Z. and W. Willett, "Changes in dietary fat and declining coronary heart disease in Poland," 231 BMJ, 2005: 187-188.

proven relationship between diets high in trans fat content and LDL ('bad') cholesterol levels..."[6] As explained below, however, FDA has not yet approved a health claim in labeling for this diet-disease relationship.

Given that heart disease is the leading cause of death in the United States, accounting for almost one-third of all deaths in 1997, the benefits of increasing consumer awareness of the risk of high saturated fat and trans fat intake are clearly substantial.[7] One important potential source for such information is health claims on package labels and in advertising for products that are lower in saturated fat or trans fat than competing products consumers might choose.

During the period 1982-1990, an increasing proportion of advertising by fats and oils producers contained claims concerning heart health. These claims were encouraged by the FTC's decision in 1982 to hold health claims to the same deception and substantiation standards that governed advertising for other goods and services.[8] By 1990, one-third of magazine advertisements for fats and oils made an explicit disease claim concerning the heart-health benefits of products lower in saturated fat, such as corn oil. An additional 12 percent of ads contained an indirect heart-health claim relating to the beneficial impact of the food on serum cholesterol levels.[9]

Figure 1 shows one such print advertisement for Puritan Oil. This ad, which ran in January 1991, provides detailed information on the saturated fat content of various fats and oils, and contains the following health claim:

---

[6]   "FDA Fact Sheet On Trans Fat Acids," July 9, 2003, available at http://www.fda.gov/oc/initiatives/transfat/q_a.html.

[7]   "US Death Statistics for 1997," Center for Disease Control, available at http://www.disastercenter.com/cdc/.

[8]   Under a longstanding liaison agreement between the agencies, FDA has primary jurisdiction over labeling claims for food products and dietary supplements, while the FTC has jurisdiction over advertising claims. Prior to 1982, the FTC was engaged in an ongoing rulemaking that proposed strict limits on all food health claims in adverstising, particularly for fats and oils. The rulemaking was terminated in December 1982. During the 1980s, FDA also adopted a more lenient enforcement posture toward food health claims in labeling. In particular, the agency failed to challenge a large-scale labeling and advertising campaign that Kellogg began in October 1984 for its high-fiber cereals. Kellogg claimed that diets high in fiber could reduce the risk of certain kinds of cancer. In 1987, FDA formally proposed a rule that would have based labeling regulation on an *ex post* deception standard.

[9]   *See* Ippolito, P., and J. Pappalardo, "Advertising Nutrition & Health," Bureau of Economics Staff Report, Federal Trade Commission, September 2002: 151-153.

Figure 1
Pre-NLEA Heart-Health Advertisement

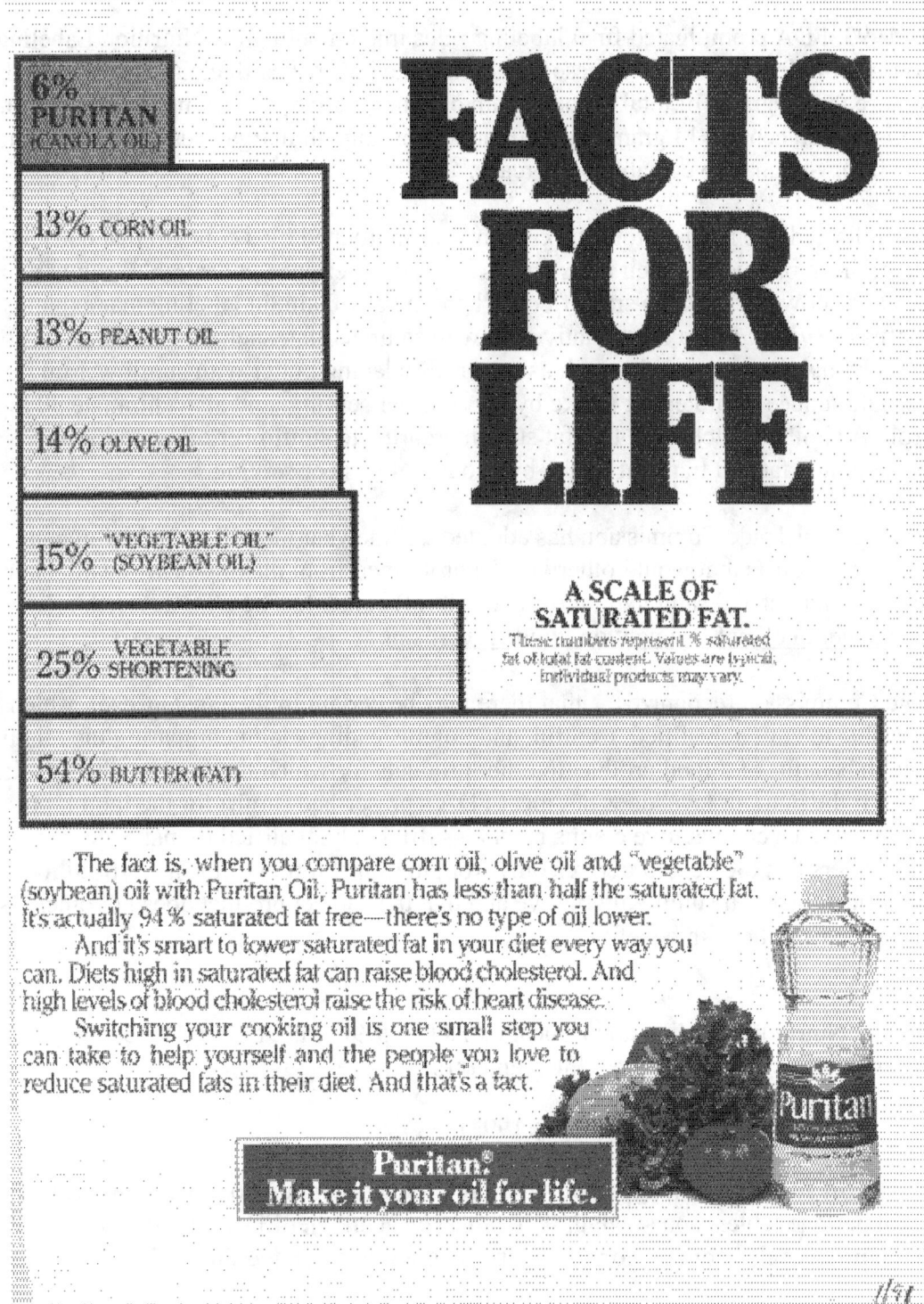

And it's smart to lower saturated fat in your diet every way you can. Diets high in saturated fat can raise blood cholesterol. And high levels of blood cholesterol raise the risk of heart disease.

In 1993, FDA promulgated final labeling rules implementing the Nutrition Labeling and Education Act of 1990 (NLEA).[10] These rules prohibited heart-health claims for any food that contains more than 3 grams of total fat or 1 gram of saturated fat per serving.[11] This eliminated cooking oils, which contain 14 grams of total fat per serving, all margarines (11 grams of total fat per serving), and many vegetable oil spreads.[12]

As indicated, the limit on total fat content was motivated by a concern that consumers might add high-fat products to their diets and as a result experience undesirable weight gain. This regulation, however, had the side effect of banning any claim in labeling that explains the heart benefits of *substituting* a food relatively low in saturated fat, such as sunflower oil, for a food relatively high in saturated fat, such as butter. Replacing butter with sunflower oil in cooking would reduce saturated fat intake by 6 grams per serving, and also eliminate 30 mg of cholesterol. A similar switch from full-fat stick margarine to sunflower oil would lower combined saturated fat and trans fat intake by about 5 grams per serving.

The Federal Trade Commission has adopted a somewhat more flexible enforcement posture toward products that would otherwise be prohibited from making heart-health claims by FDA limits on total fat and saturated fat (or cholesterol) content. The FTC advised in its May 1994 Enforcement Policy Statement on Food Advertising:

> The Commission recognizes ... that there may be certain limited instances in which it is possible to craft a qualified, truthful, and nonmisleading claim comparing the relative health benefits of a food product to other products for which the food can be substituted, even if the nutrient level does not meet FDA's prescribed (limit) for the food .... In addition, such comparative claims must be sufficiently qualified to make clear to consumers that the benefit derives only from the substitution of the advertised food for a significantly less healthful alternative and that the subject product does not otherwise offer an overall health benefit.[13]

---

[10] Nutrition Labeling and Education Act of 1990, Pub. L. No. 101-535, 104 Stat. 2353 (codified in part at 21 U.S.C. § 343(i), and (r)).

[11] 21 C.F.R. § 101.14(d)(2)(vi)(1993).

[12] In addition, although many of these products contain no more than one gram of saturated fat per one-tablespoon serving, they fail to meet another FDA requirement that 50 grams of the product also contain no more than one gram of saturated fat.

[13] Federal Trade Commission, Enforcement Policy Statement on Food Advertising (May 1994), Washington, D.C., pp 24-25.

Despite the greater latitude that advertisers of fats and oils have to make comparative health claims, a recent content analysis of print food advertising revealed that such claims virtually disappeared after the Statement was published and the FDA labeling rules took effect.[14] Further, use of nutrient content claims (such as "low in saturated fat"), which are allowed in labeling and advertising, also fell dramatically after 1994.[15]

It is not obvious why the FDA *labeling* rules would have such a dramatic impact on health claims in *advertising*, or why advertisers would not make greater use of nutrient content claims to highlight indirectly any heart-health advantage their products might enjoy. Perhaps advertisers interpreted the Statement's ostensibly more lenient treatment of substitution claims very cautiously, and did not think nutrient content claims concerning saturated fat content would have sufficient impact without accompanying explicit health claims that helped consumers understand the significance of reducing saturated fat intake.

In recent years, FDA has used its enforcement discretion to allow health claims for certain fats and oils that exceed the total fat limit of 3 grams. In September 2000 FDA authorized an unqualified heart-health claim for foods containing plant sterol and stanol esters.[16] This includes spreads and salad dressings with added amounts of plant stanol or sterol.

In addition, *qualified* heart-health claims have been allowed for certain tree nuts and peanuts and for olive and canola oil. FDA concluded that the scientific evidence supporting a heart-health claim for these specific foods had not yet attained the level of Significant Scientific Agreement, and therefore required the claims to specify a lower level of support.[17] Since July 2003, the following claim has been approved for use in labeling for most tree nuts and peanuts:[18]

---

[14]   Ippolito and Pappalardo, *op cit*. The authors examined the number and types of nutrient content and health claims made in a sample of over 11,000 ads in eight women's and general readership magazines over the period 1977 to 1997.

[15]   *Id.*, p. 157. The percentage of ads with such claims fell from a high of 53 percent in 1990 to 8.3 percent in 1997.

[16]   65 Fed. Reg. 54686 (2000). *See also* "FDA Authorizes New Coronary Heart Disease Health Claim for Plant Sterol and Plant Stanol Esters," available at http://www.cfsan.fda.gov/~lrd/tpsterol.html.

[17]   The approved claims were intended to convey a "B" level of scientific certainty, which is the first level below Significant Scientific Agreement.

[18]   *See* "Qualified Health Claims: Letter of Enforcement Discretion–Nuts and Coronary Heart Disease," U.S. Food and Drug Administration, Office of Nutritional Products, Labeling, and Dietary Supplements, July 14, 2003, available at http://www.cfsan.fda.gov/~dms/qhcnuts2.html.

Scientific evidence suggests but does not prove that eating 1.5 ounces per day of most nuts [such as *name of specific nut*] as part of a diet low in saturated fat and cholesterol may reduce the risk of heart disease.

In November 2004, FDA approved the following qualified claim for foods that contain 6 grams or more of olive oil:[19]

Limited and not conclusive scientific evidence suggests that eating about 2 tablespoons (23 grams) of olive oil daily may reduce the risk of coronary heart disease due to the monounsaturated fat in olive oil. To achieve this possible benefit, olive oil is to replace a similar amount of saturated fat and not increase the total number of calories you eat in a day. One serving of this product [*Name of food*] contains [*x*] grams of olive oil.

FDA approved a similarly worded qualified claim for canola oil in October 2006.[20] To date, however, a broad range of cooking oils and vegetable spreads that are high in polyunsaturated or monounsaturated fat still cannot make any health claims in labeling. Further, those products that have obtained approval to make *qualified* heart-health claims for a particular type of cooking cannot make any *unqualified* claims (such as those used in our research) that link heart health more generally to diets low in saturated fat.

Finally, irrespective of saturated fat content, no food that has been formulated to reduce or eliminate trans fatty acids can explain in labeling the heart-health benefits of restricting consumption of this type of fat, or use nutrient content descriptors (such as "low") to spotlight advantageously low levels of trans fat. FDA has concluded that it currently lacks a scientific basis for establishing a "Daily Recommended Value" for trans fat intake, and absent such a determination the agency is not willing to establish standards for nutrient content claims or for health claims.[21]

---

[19] *See* Letter Responding to Health Claim Petition dated August 28, 2003: Monounsaturated Fatty Acids from Olive Oil and Coronary Heart Disease, U.S. Food and Drug Administration, CFSAN, November 1, 2004, available at http://www.cfsan.fda.gov/~dms/qhcnuts2.html.

[20] *See* "Qualified Health claims: Letter of Enforcement Discretion-Unsaturated Fatty Acids from Canola Oil and Reduced Risk of Coronary Heart Disease," U.S. Food and Drug Administration, Office of Nutritional Products, Labeling, and Dietary Supplements, October 6, 2006, available at http://www.cfsan.fda.gov/~dms/qhccanol.html.

[21] *See* "FDA/CFSAN: Questions and Answers about Trans Fat Nutrition Labeling" available at http://www.cfsan.fda.gov/~dms/qatrans2.html.

III. Experimental Design

Our research employed standard mall-intercept copy test methodology to measure respondents reactions to twelve print ad treatments for two products. The first product was a fictitious cooking oil, "Sunflower Fields," that contained only one gram of saturated fat (and, like all cooking oils, 14 grams of total fat) per one-tablespoon serving. The second product, "Sunrise Spread," was a fictitious vegetable spread in stick form that contained no trans fatty acids, but 10 grams of total fat per one-tablespoon serving. A total of 1,200 respondents participated in the research, with 100 respondents assigned to each of the twelve print ad treatments.

Interviews were conducted by Cunningham Sensory Services ("Cunningham") in five geographically dispersed shopping malls.[22] Potential participants were approached while shopping and screened for eligibility. Subjects were required to be the primary grocery shopper and to have purchased a cooking oil or vegetable spread or margarine for themselves or a family member during the past 30 days. Respondents were selected so that the final sample would be 75% female, with ages evenly distributed across four categories: 21-29, 30-39, 40-49, and 50 and above. Consenting shoppers were then taken to an interview room where the questionnaire was administered.

Cunningham interviewers entered participant responses directly into a computerized data base during the questioning, which allowed very short turnaround times for data analysis. We took advantage of this capability to stage testing of the various ad treatments in several waves. The composition of subsequent waves was guided by the results obtained from the earlier testing. As detailed below, this procedure avoided needless repetition of any language or disclosures that had already proven ineffective or unnecessary, and freed up cells for testing more promising approaches.

A. Ad Treatments in Detail

. Table 1 summarizes the key claims in and differences among the various Sunflower Fields and Sunrise Spread treatments. Figures 2-13 present the entire ads as they appeared to respondents. The first ad treatments featured the fictitious Sunflower Fields cooking oil. A "Tombstone Control" ad was included to measure the prior beliefs that respondents brought with them concerning the nutrient profile of cooking oils. That treatment, which is shown in Figure 2, contains no information relating to fat content or any other nutrient, and no health claim other than any implied claim that might be conveyed by the product name. The ad merely announces the availability of Sunflower Fields, and mentions its possible uses and its fresh taste. Accordingly, any opinions that respondents give about the product's nutrient profile or healthiness represent their prior beliefs about a cooking oil of this type.

The second Sunflower Fields treatment, shown in Figure 3, is designed to determine how

---

[22]   These malls were located in Arlington (Virginia), Seattle, Jacksonville (Florida), Los Angeles, and Dallas.

consumer impressions of the product change when information is provided on nutrient content. This ad specifies that Sunflower Fields contains one gram of saturated fat per one-tablespoon serving, and features a prominent banner at the top of the bottle identifying the cooking oil as "Low in Saturated Fat." This ad treatment does not explain the health significance of using products that are low in saturated fat.

It should be noted that the ad does not suggest that Sunflower Fields should be used as a *substitute* for other similar products that are higher in saturated fat. It merely asks readers to "...try new Sunflower Fields today." This treatment tests whether consumers interpret such ad copy to suggest that the product should be used as an *addition* to an existing diet. The ad will be referenced as the "Nutrient Content Simple" treatment.

Figure 4 shows the next treatment, which is also limited to nutrient content information, but promotes Sunflower Fields explicitly as a substitute for less healthy alternatives. The relevant ad copy reads: "So, if you're still cooking with butter, margarine, or regular vegetable oil, switch to new Sunflower Fields today." Because product use is presented in the context of a dietary substitution, the ad will be referenced as the "Nutrient Content Substitution" treatment. The ad is included to determine whether the substitution language will reduce any unwarranted halo effect that the information on saturated fat content might have on respondent perceptions of the product's calorie or total fat content.

The next two treatments, shown in Figures 5 and 6, are referenced as the "Health Claim Simple" and "Health Claim Substitution" ads, respectively. They parallel the construction of the third and fourth treatments, but an explicit hearth-health claim is inserted between the nutrient content information and the final sentence. In both cases, the health claim reads: "And that's great news, because diets low in saturated fat can reduce the risk of heart disease!" Results from these ads can be compared with the corresponding nutrient content ad to gauge the marginal impact on consumer perceptions of adding the explicit heart-health information.

An additional treatment was included to determine the impact of a health claim standing alone, without any information on saturated fat content. This "Health Claim Control" ad is shown in Figure 7. The first paragraph is identical to the Tombstone Control ad. The second paragraph is taken *verbatim* from the Health Claim Substitution treatment. Of interest is whether a health claim by itself will have a greater effect on consumer perceptions than a simple nutrient content claim. Figure 8 presents the last Sunflower Fields treatment, referenced as the "Calorie Disclosure." It is identical to the Nutrient Content Simple ad, but includes an asterisked disclosure stating the number of calories in one tablespoon of Sunflower Fields (120).

Testing of the Sunrise Spread treatments did not begin until the results from the Sunflower Fields ads had been analyzed in August 2004. As detailed below, these results suggested that respondents were not drawing any important distinctions between the "substitution" and "simple" variations of the nutrient content and health claim ads. Although we

10

Table 1 Summary of Advertising Treatments

Ad Treatment	Nutrient Content Claim	Health Claim	Substitution Context	Other Disclosure	Figure
Sunflower Fields Sunflower Oil Ads					
	Low in sat. fat; 1 gram per tbsp	*Reduce the risk of heart disease*	*.. still cooking w/ butter, etc., switch ...*		
Tombstone Control					2
Nutrient Content Claim: Simple	✓				3
Nutrient Content Claim: Substitution	✓		✓		4
Health Claim: Simple	✓	✓			5
Health Claim: Substitution	✓	✓	✓		6
Health Claim: Control		✓	✓		7
Nutrient Content Claim: Calorie Disclosure	✓			Calories per tbsp = 120	8
Sunrise Spread Ads					
	No trans fatty acids.	*Reduce the risk of heart disease*			
Tombstone Control					9
Nutrient Content: Simple	✓				10
Health Claim: Simple	✓	✓			11
Nutrient Content Claim: Calorie Disclosure	✓			Calories per tbsp = 90	12
Nutrient Content Claim: Fat Disclosure	✓			Fat per tbsp = 10 grams	13

<u>Figure 2</u>
Sunflower Fields Tombstone Control

Announcing new *Sunflower Fields* cooking oil! Now appearing at a supermarket near you.

New *Sunflower Fields* sunflower oil is perfect for salads and cooking. And now it tastes fresher than ever. Pick up a bottle today!

For recipe ideas, visit us at www.sunflowerfields.com.

<u>Figure 3</u>
Sunflower Fields Nutrient Content Simple

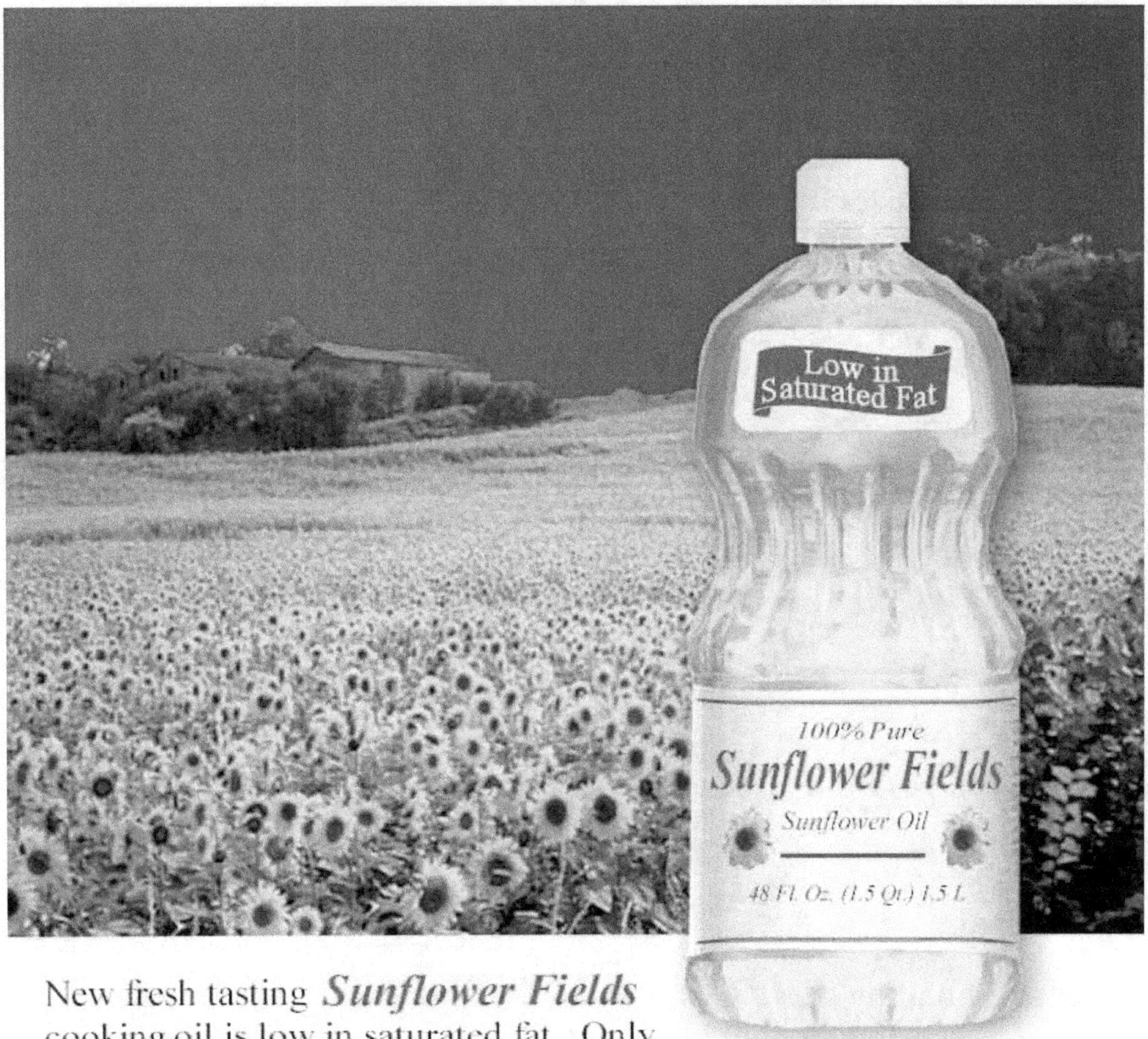
Low in Saturated Fat
100% Pure
Sunflower Fields
Sunflower Oil
48 Fl. Oz. (1.5 Qt.) 1.5 L
New fresh tasting Sunflower Fields cooking oil is low in saturated fat. Only one gram of saturated fat per one Tbsp serving!
So try new Sunflower Fields today. Now appearing at a supermarket near you!
For recipe ideas, visit us at www.sunflowerfields.com.

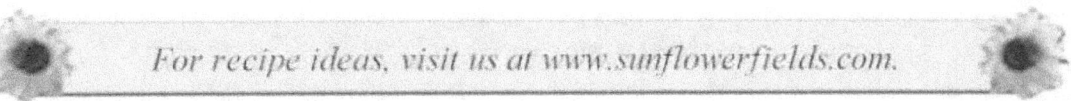

Figure 4
Sunflower Fields Nutrient Content Substitution

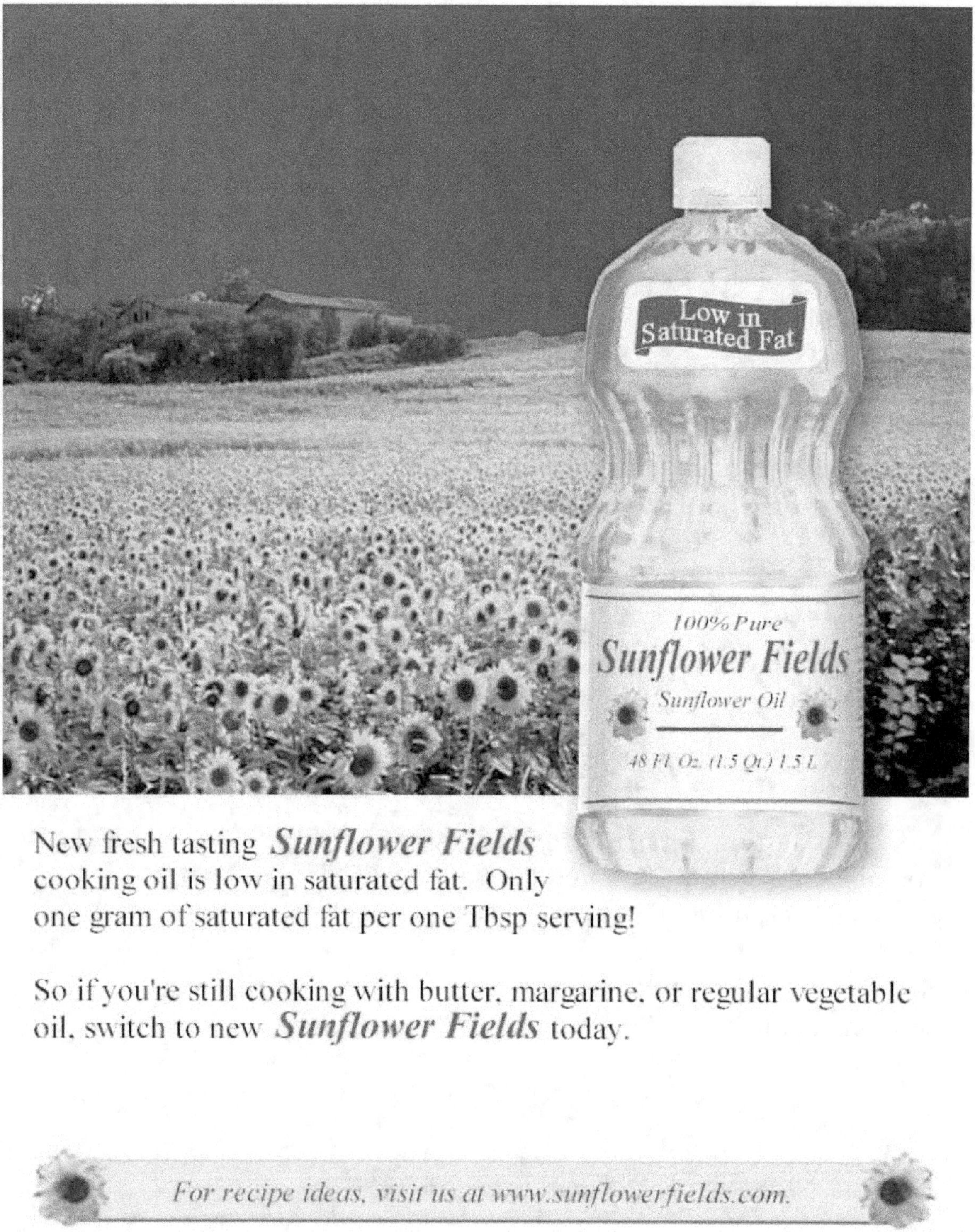

New fresh tasting *Sunflower Fields* cooking oil is low in saturated fat. Only one gram of saturated fat per one Tbsp serving!

So if you're still cooking with butter, margarine, or regular vegetable oil, switch to new *Sunflower Fields* today.

For recipe ideas, visit us at www.sunflowerfields.com.

Figure 5
Sunflower Fields Health Claim Simple

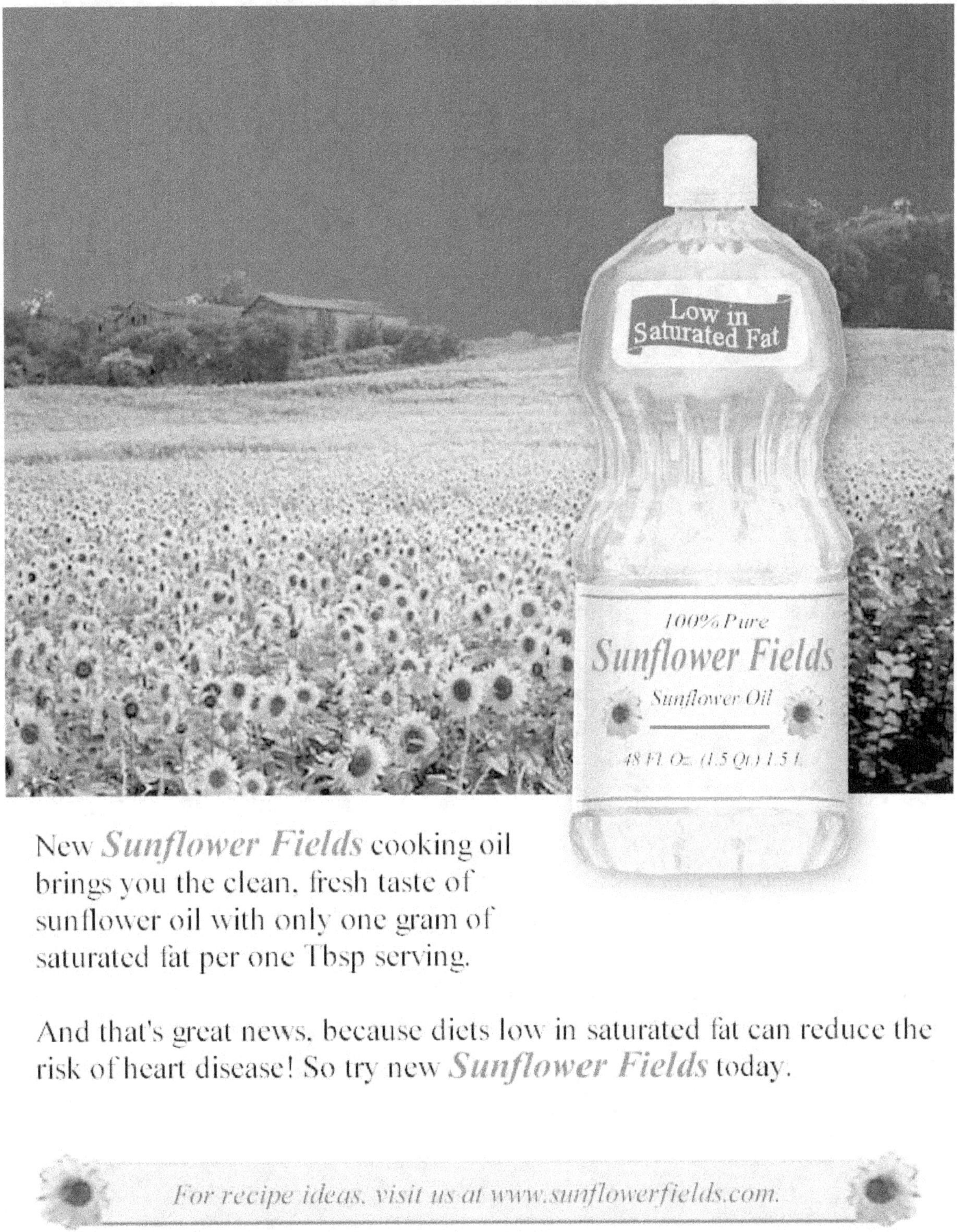

Low in Saturated Fat
100% Pure
Sunflower Fields
Sunflower Oil
48 Fl. Oz. (1.5 Qt) 1.5 L
New Sunflower Fields cooking oil brings you the clean, fresh taste of sunflower oil with only one gram of saturated fat per one Tbsp serving.
And that's great news, because diets low in saturated fat can reduce the risk of heart disease! So try new Sunflower Fields today.
For recipe ideas, visit us at www.sunflowerfields.com.

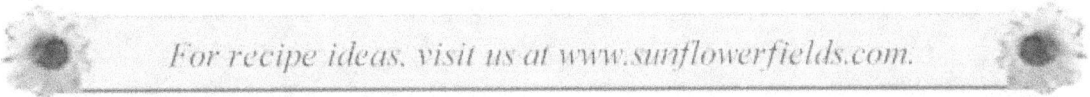

Figure 6
Sunflower Fields Health Claim Substitution

New fresh tasting *Sunflower Fields*
cooking oil is low in saturated fat. Only
one gram of saturated fat per one Tbsp serving!

And that's great news, because diets low in saturated fat can reduce the
risk of heart disease! So if you're still cooking with butter, margarine,
or regular vegetable oil, switch to new *Sunflower Fields* today.

For recipe ideas, visit us at www.sunflowerfields.com.

Figure 7
Sunflower Fields Health Claim Control

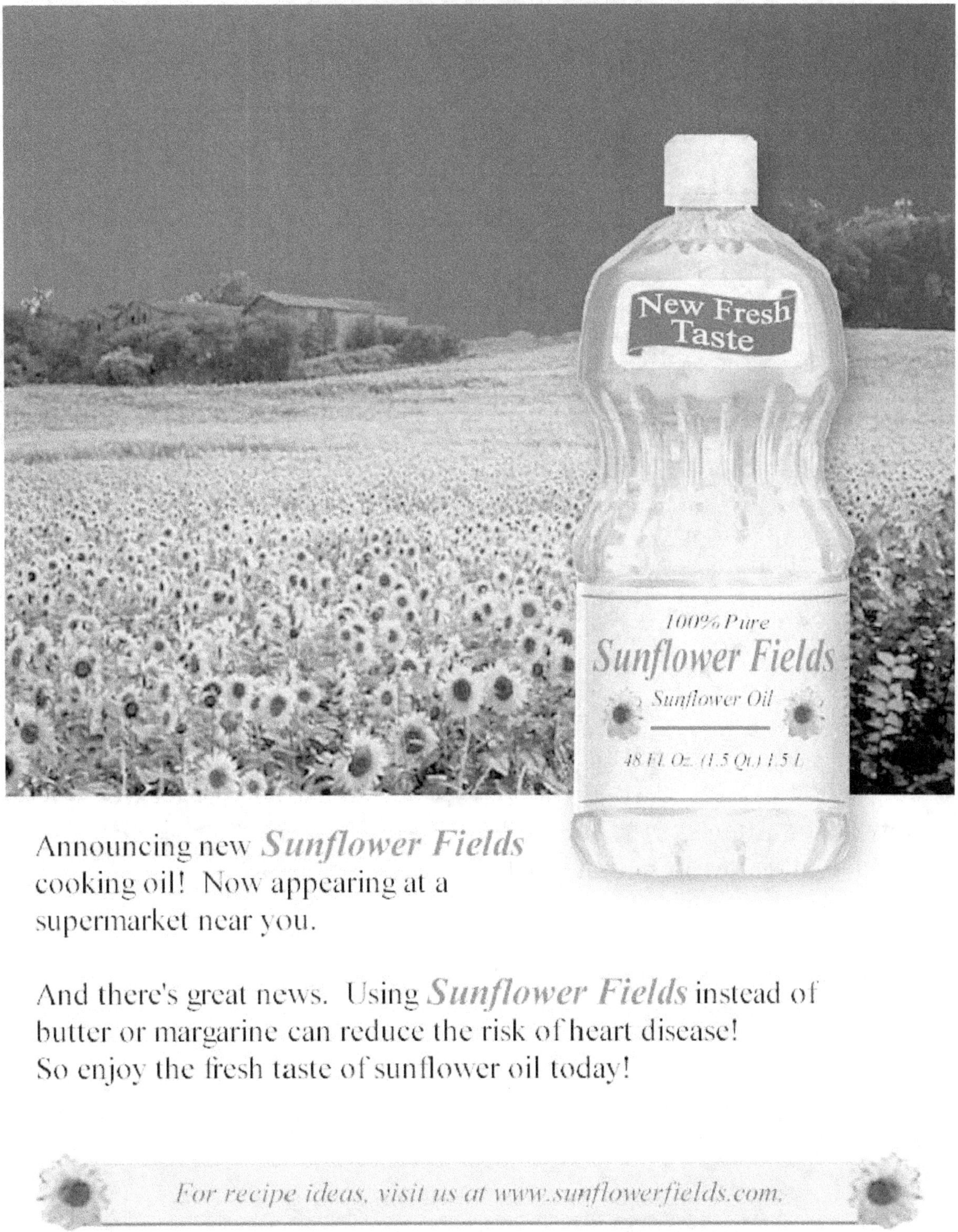

Announcing new *Sunflower Fields* cooking oil! Now appearing at a supermarket near you.

And there's great news. Using *Sunflower Fields* instead of butter or margarine can reduce the risk of heart disease! So enjoy the fresh taste of sunflower oil today!

For recipe ideas, visit us at www.sunflowerfields.com.

Figure 8
Sunflower Fields Calorie Disclosure

New fresh tasting *Sunflower Fields*
cooking oil is low in saturated fat. Only
one gram of saturated fat per one Tbsp serving!*

So try new *Sunflower Fields* today. Now appearing at a
supermarket near you!

*Calories per Tbsp: 120.

For recipe ideas, visit us at www.sunflowerfields.com.

could not be sure that readers of these versions of the Sunrise Spread treatments would also fail to draw any distinctions, budgetary constraints dictated that we eliminate two of the treatments used in the Sunflower Fields testing. Accordingly, we only tested the "simple" language for the Sunrise Spread advertisements. In addition, the "Health Claim Control" treatment was also eliminated to free up a cell for testing an additional remedy disclosure. This left a total of five test cells for the Sunrise Spread product.

Figure 9 displays the Tombstone Control treatment. The only information presented concerns the product's taste and possible uses. The Nutrient Content Simple ad is shown in Figure 10. The text states rather emphatically that Sunrise Spread contains no trans fatty acids, but does not link this fact to a heart-health benefit. The explicit heart-health claim, along with the nutrient content information, is contained in the Health Claim Simple ad, shown in Figure 11. The package shown in the ad sports a prominent heart symbol to further differentiate this treatment from the nutrient content version. The Calorie Disclosure is shown in Figure 12. It follows the same format as the corresponding Sunflower Fields ad, except that the number of calories in a tablespoon of Sunrise Spread is 90 rather than 120.

Finally, Figure 13 presents an alternative remedy treatment that discloses the total fat in one serving of Sunrise Spread instead of the number of calories. Earlier testing of the Sunflower Fields Calorie Disclosure indicated that many respondents did not consider 120 calories per serving as a negative product attribute. Although the heart-health concern posed by these products relates to their caloric density rather than their high total fat content *per se*, we wished to test whether respondents might regard the amount of fat in Sunrise Spread–10 grams per serving–as a greater cause for concern than the number of calories

B. Questionnaire Design

The questionnaires for Sunflower Fields and Sunrise Spread were very similar, although a question was added to the Sunrise Spread questionnaire in an attempt to focus respondents more directly on the issue of possible weight gain from liberal use of the product. In both cases, the questionnaire followed a classic "funneling" structure. Respondents initially were asked in completely open-ended fashion for their general take-away from the ad, and then were asked gradually more pointed questions that narrowed in on the key research issues. The main questionnaire for the Sunrise Spread ads is presented in Appendix A.

Respondents were allowed to see the relevant test ad twice. After the first viewing, the ad was removed from sight and the respondent was asked to identify the name of the advertised product. The respondent was then allowed to read the ad again, after which the ad was removed from sight for the remainder of the session. Interviews were terminated if a subject could not correctly identify the name of the advertised product after a second exposure (or in the case of Sunflower Fields, at least include the phrase "sunflower" or "sunflower oil" in the response). Virtually all of the respondents passed the identification test after the second exposure.

19

Figure 9
Sunrise Spread Tombstone

One taste and you'll agree. New Sunrise Spread is as fresh as a country morning.

It's perfect for cooking and baking, or try it melted on a slice of hot toast.

Pick up a box of new Sunrise Spread today! Now appearing at a supermarket near you.

For recipe ideas, visit us at www.sunrisespread.com.

Figure 10
Sunrise Spread Nutrient Content Simple

We kept the same country fresh taste. But we took OUT the trans fatty acids.

That's right. New Sunrise Spread contains no trans fatty acids. Zero.

So pick up a box of new Sunrise Spread today!

For recipe ideas, visit us at www.sunrisespread.com.

Figure 11
Sunrise Spread Health Claim Simple

We kept the same country fresh taste. But we took OUT the trans fatty acids.

That's right. New Sunrise Spread contains no trans fatty acids. Zero.

And that's great news, because diets low in trans fatty acids can reduce the risk of heart disease.

So pick up a box of new Sunrise Spread today!

For recipe ideas, visit us at www.sunrisespread.com.

Figure 12
Sunrise Spread Calorie Disclosure

We kept the same country fresh taste. But we took OUT the trans fatty acids.

That's right. New Sunrise Spread contains no trans fatty acids. Zero.*

So pick up a box of new Sunrise Spread today!

*Calories per Tbsp: 90

For recipe ideas, visit us at www.sunrisespread.com.

Figure 13
Sunrise Spread Total Fat Disclosure

We kept the same country fresh taste. But we took OUT the trans fatty acids.

That's right. New Sunrise Spread contains no trans fatty acids. Zero. *

So pick up a box of new Sunrise Spread today!

* Total Fat per Tbsp: 10 grams

For recipe ideas, visit us at www.sunrisespread.com.

The exact wording of the test questions will be given in the results section below. Here we merely state the general nature of the questions to illustrate overall structure and focus of the interview. As indicated, the first question was open-ended and simply asked respondents for the main ideas that the ad communicated to them. Respondents were then asked a series of close-ended questions about ad communication, the first of which asked whether the ad said or suggested anything about Sunflower Fields (Sunrise Spread) being healthy for the heart. It originally was anticipated that most respondents seeing the nutrient content treatments would construe the references to saturated fat or trans fatty acids as implied heart-health claims, and reply positively to the question even though there were no explicit heart-health claims in the ads. Pretesting of the questionnaire demonstrated, however, that virtually all respondents interpreted the question quite narrowly and reported no heart-health claim in the nutrient content ads.

This meant that no further questions regarding heart health could be asked if such questions were confined to ad communication. It would not have been legitimate to ask what the ad said or suggested about any aspect of heart health if respondents saw no health message in the first instance. We therefore decided to broaden the scope of subsequent questions to include respondents' personal beliefs.[23] This was accomplished by prefacing the subsequent series of questions with these instructions:

> So far I have been asking you to answer questions based just on what the ad said or suggested. Now I would like you to answer the following questions based on what the ad said or suggested, or on anything else you may know or believe.

There followed a series of five questions that explored from different vantage points whether respondents understood that the product in question could contribute to weight gain and associated heart problems if consumed without discretion. The first of these asked respondents to assume they added Sunflower Fields or Sunrise Spread to their regular diets without making any other changes in what they ate. (Examples were given illustrating how this might occur.) Respondents were then asked to rate how healthy such an addition would be using a seven-point scale that ranged from "extremely bad for the heart," to "extremely good for the heart." Although there is no single correct answer to this question, presumably any response indicating a positive effect on heart health could be considered incorrect.

---

[23]   The shift to beliefs also increased the usefulness of the Tombstone Control as a reference point for determining the incremental impact of the explicit nutrient content and health claims in the test ads. Since the Tombstone Control did not contain any nutrient content or health information, very few respondents would have taken away a nutrient or health message from the ad. Most respondents therefore could not have been questioned further on relevant ad communication issues, which effectively would have precluded meaningful comparisons between the Tombstone Control and other ad treatments. Posing the questions in terms of personal beliefs greatly increased response rates and provided a more powerful statistical test for detecting differences in belief-based response patterns associated with the addition of nutrient content and health claims.

Next, respondents were asked to use the same scale to indicate the heart-health impact of substituting the oil (spread) for butter in cooking. Respondents who understood that butter is substantially higher in saturated fat and cholesterol than the advertised product would be expected to rate this dietary substitution as healthier than simply adding the oil or spread to the diet.

In a variation on this theme, respondents were next given three possible menu choices: (1) a filet of fish that had been baked with only lemon juice for liquid and seasoning; (2) a fish filet pan-fried in Sunflower Fields or Sunrise Spread, with lemon juice for seasoning; and (3) a fish filet pan-fried in butter or traditional stick margarine, again with only lemon juice as seasoning. Respondents were then asked which of the three choices would be best for the heart, and then which of the remaining two alternatives would be better for the heart. Again, the key to arranging the choices in the correct order (with the relatively low-calorie baking method first, and the butter-fried option last) would be understanding that the oil and spread products are calorically dense despite their otherwise positive fat profile.

Following analysis of the results from the series of Sunflower Fields ads, a question was added to the Sunrise Spread questionnaire to deal more explicitly with the effect regular use of the product might have on weight gain *per se*, rather than the more indirect impact the product might have on heart health. Respondents were asked to use a seven-point scale to rate how good regular use of the product would be for losing weight. The choices ranged from "extremely bad for losing weight" to "extremely good for losing weight."

The questioning then shifted to a direct focus on the caloric content of the advertised products. Respondents were first asked to compare the number of calories in one tablespoon of Sunflower Fields or Sunrise Spread with the number in one tablespoon of butter. A five-point scale was provided, with values ranging from "much higher in calories than butter" to "much lower in calories than butter." For Sunflower Fields, the correct answer was "somewhat higher in calories than butter," since cooking oils are entirely fat and contain 120 calories per 14-gram serving (one tablespoon), while butter and stick margarine have about 11 grams of fat per serving, which corresponds to 100 calories. For Sunrise Spread, which contains 90 calories per serving, the correct answer could be either "about equal in calories to butter" or "somewhat lower in calories than butter.

Finally, respondents were asked directly to estimate the absolute number of calories in a serving of Sunflower Fields or Sunrise Spread. Five ranges were provided: more than 200, 151-200, 101-150, 51-100, and 0-50. The remainder of the questionnaire included a standard purchase interest question and demographic questions concerning education and income level. Respondents were also asked whether or not they had been on a diet to lose weight at any time during the last year.

IV. Results

Our analysis of the copy test results begins with a discussion of the unprompted answers respondents gave to the initial open-ended question that asked for the main points communicated by the test ad, and then moves to the close-ended questions that are designed to address the three key research issues described earlier. The discussion closes with an analysis of the responses to the purchase interest and demographic questions.

A. Open-Ended Responses

As indicated, the first question was completely open-ended and asked for the main ideas communicated by the test ad.

1. Nutrient Content Information

Not surprisingly, virtually no respondents seeing the Tombstone Control treatments for either product took away a nutrient content claim (or a health claim) as a main point of the ad. Most of the responses related to taste, availability, or possible uses in cooking. Five Sunflower Fields treatments contained nutrient content information (and, for two, a health claim as well). From 44 percent (Calorie Disclosure) to 65.3 percent (Nutrient Content Simple) of respondents gave "less" or "one gram" saturated fat as a main point of the ad. Interestingly, however, from about one-fifth to one-third of respondents mentioned "less" or "one gram" *fat* as a main message. This is a possible indication that some consumers confused saturated fat with total fat. It is also interesting that 25 percent of respondents in the Sunflower Fields Calorie Disclosure test cell thought the ad communicated a message of "less calories." No respondents placed the calorie information in a negative context.

Results for the four Sunrise Spread treatments with nutrient content information were quite similar. The proportion of respondents mentioning "no" or "less" trans fatty acids ranged from 58 percent to 73 percent. From 15 percent to 25 percent of respondents referenced a lack of "fat" as the main message, again suggesting some confusion concerning the total fat profile of the product. Unlike the Sunflower Fields Calorie Disclosure results, only 10 percent of respondents in the corresponding Sunrise Spread cell reported that the ad conveyed a "less" calories message.

2. Health Information

For the Sunflower Fields Health Claim Control treatment, which mentioned only a heart-health benefit with no information on nutrient content, over half of the respondents referenced the claimed heart-health benefit explicitly, and about one-third used more general terms, such as "healthy for you." (There was no corresponding ad treatment for Sunrise Spread.) Two of the remaining Sunflower Fields ads contained a health claim (and nutrient content disclosures). About one-half of respondents listed a specific heart-health claim or a general health message as a main point of the ad. Forty-three percent of respondents seeing the only Sunrise Spread treatment with a health claim mentioned a health message. When compared with the greater playback of nutrient content messages, these percentages suggest that the nutrient content information in the Sunflower Fields and Sunrise Spread ads was somewhat more salient to respondents than the additional health claim.

B. Responses to Close-Ended Questions

The first close-ended question of interest asked respondents if the test ad said or suggested anything about whether Sunflower Fields oil (Sunrise Spread) was healthy for your heart. The results confirmed earlier predictions from the pre-testing that respondents would fail to see an implied health claim in the ads that contained only nutrient content information about levels of saturated fat or trans fatty acids in the advertised product.

For the two Sunflower Fields nutrient content ads (the Simple and Substitution ads) only 11 percent and 15 percent of respondents, respectively, stated that the ad said or suggested anything about the product being healthy for the heart. For the Calorie Disclosure, this figure *rose* somewhat to 22 percent, indicating again that some respondents interpreted the number of calories in Sunflower Fields (120 calories per serving) in a positive light. Three Sunrise Spread ads contained nutrient content information but no direct health claim. These were the Nutrient Content Simple, Calorie, and Total Fat treatments, which recorded positive responses of 17 percent, 13 percent, and 8 percent, respectively for the heart-health ad meaning question.

Had the subsequent questions concerning heart health been based on ad communication rather than beliefs, the study would have failed to gather useful results for any of these ads. Consequently, as explained earlier, all of the respondents at this point were instructed instead to base their answers to subsequent questions either on what the ad said or suggested, *or* on anything else they might know or believe.

1. Heart-Healthiness of Adding Product to the Diet

The first of these "beliefs" questions for Sunflower Fields oil asked respondents:

Suppose you added Sunflower Fields to your regular diet without making any other changes in what you eat. For example, suppose you started using more dressing on your salad than you used to. Do you think that adding Sunflower Fields to your diet would be (1) extremely bad for the heart, (2) bad for the heart, (3) somewhat bad for the heart, (4) neither bad nor good for the heart, (5) somewhat good for the heart, (6) good for the heart, or (7) extremely good for the heart?

The corresponding question for Sunrise Spread used as an illustration of a dietary addition: "For example, suppose that in the past you didn't use any spread or butter on your toast or sandwiches, but now you start using Sunrise Spread on them."

Consumers who understood the total fat and calorie profile of these products, and who also understood the effect of weight gain on heart health, might be expected to choose a score below the mid-point rating of 4.0 ("neither bad nor good for the heart.). The Tombstone Control results would reveal respondents' prior beliefs concerning ordinary cooking oil and vegetable spreads that did not promote favorable levels of saturated fat or trans fatty acids. Irrespective of the absolute level of the score for the Tombstone Control, we would expect the average rating to increase in the nutrient content and health claim test conditions. Respondents seeing the nutrient and/or health claims might conclude with justification that adding the advertised oil or spread to the diet would be health*ier* for the heart than adding an ordinary oil or spread that contained more saturated fat or trans fats. Thus, by itself, this increase would not necessarily indicate that the claims had misled consumers concerning the nutrient profile or other heart-health properties of the advertised products.

Any such increase in average ratings would be more problematic, however, if the initial score for the Tombstone Control were below the midpoint, but then increased to above the midpoint in any of the nutrient content or health claim test cells. This increase would then indicate that the nutrient or health information had misled consumers into thinking that the advertised products had properties that contributed to hearth health simply by their presence in the diet.

Figure 14 shows the mean responses for the various Sunflower Fields ads. Table 2 summarizes the statistical significance levels for the key differences in means between treatments. The average scores for all of the treatments are above the midpoint, and generally are above, or close to, "Somewhat good for the heart." The underlying reasons for this perception of the product cannot be isolated at this point. Perhaps respondents did not understand the precise meaning of the phrase "adding to the diet," and were still thinking of the cooking oil as a substitute for other fats and oils. Alternatively, many respondents may have viewed Sunflower Fields as low or moderately low in total fat and calories. As will be discussed below, results from subsequent questions help to resolve this issue.

The lowest score–4.63–was recorded by the tombstone control ad, which establishes the baseline beliefs that respondents brought with them to the test. The mean score of 5.06 for the Nutrient Content Simple ad is significantly higher than the Tombstone control score (P=.025), indicating that the information on saturated fat content did have a positive impact on respondents' evaluation of the heart benefit of adding the cooking oil to the diet. Although the rating for the Nutrient Content Substitution ad is slightly below the Nutrient Content Simple ad, the difference is not significant. This suggests that placing the ad claim in the context of a dietary substitution does not alert consumers to a possible downside from simply adding the product to the diet.

The mean ratings for the three ads with explicit heart-health claims are very similar, ranging from 5.21 to 5.30, and are statistically indistinguishable. As a group, the health claim treatments score higher than the nutrient content claims, and are significantly higher than the Tombstone Control ratings. With the exception of the Health Claim Control ad, however, there

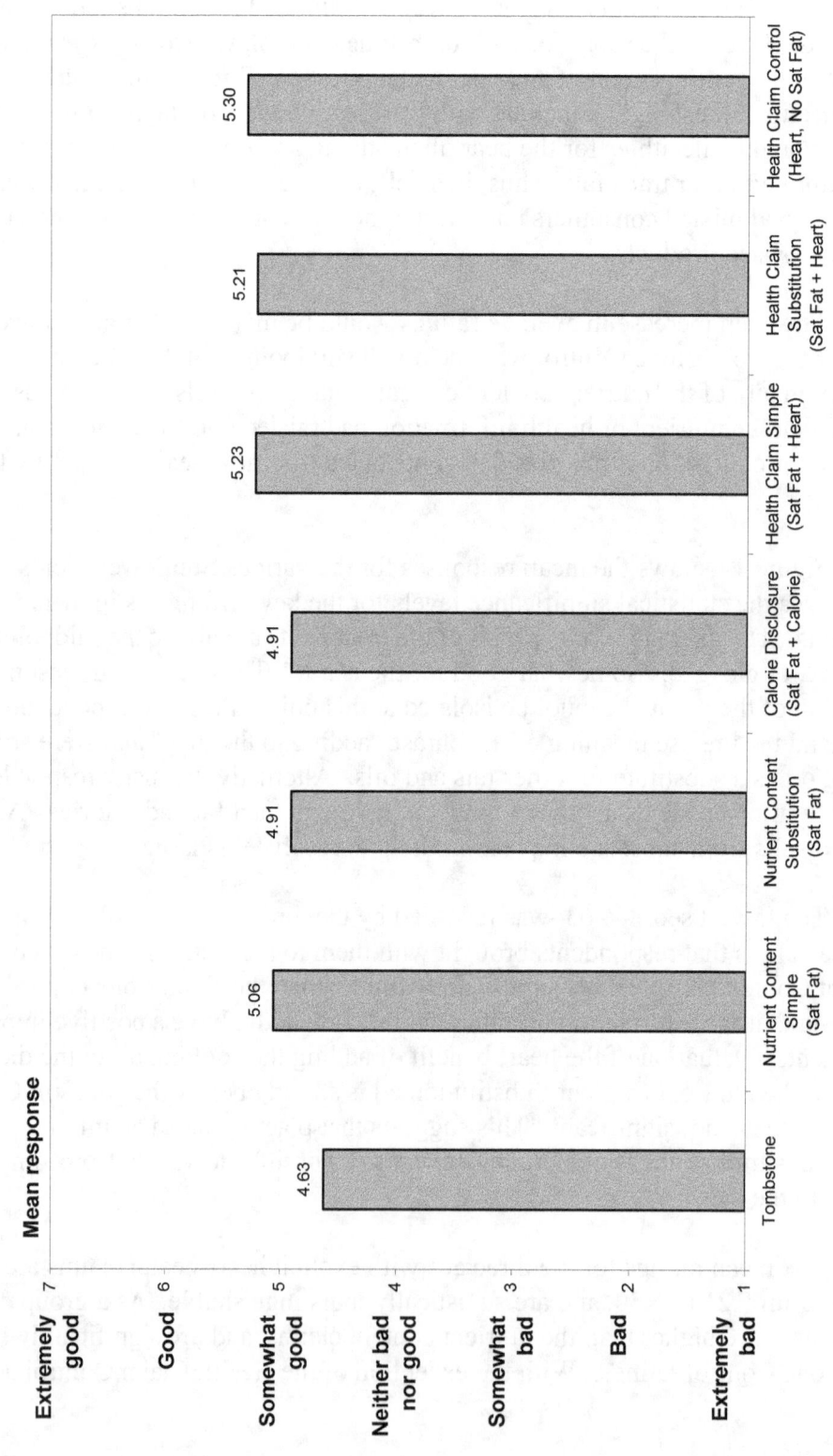

Figure 14
Sunflower Fields
Heart-Health Effect of Adding to Diet

30

Table 2 Mean Consumer Response for Heart Benefits of Adding Sunflower Fields Oil to Diet[1]

Ad Treatment	Mean Response	Significant compared to Tombstone Control[2]	Significant compared to Simple Nutrient Content Claim[2]
Tombstone Control	4.63	---	
Nutrient Content Claim: Simple	5.06	**	---
Nutrient Content Claim: Substitution	4.91	**	No
Nutrient Content Claim: Calorie Disclosure	4.91	**	No
Health Claim: Simple	5.23	**	No
Health Claim: Substitution	5.21	**	No
Health Claim: Control	5.30	**	**

Notes. [1] Consumers were asked "Suppose you added Sunflower Fields to your regular diet without making any other changes in what you eat. For example, suppose you started using more dressing on your salad than you used to. Do you think that adding Sunflower Fields to your diet would be extremely bad for the heart, ..., extremely good for the heart?" Consumers were shown a card with seven choices including the indicated endpoints. See question 7 of questionnaire in Appendix A.
[2] Dashes indicate the comparison ad for the test. ** indicates significance at the 5 percent level in a simple difference-in-means t-test. *No* indicates that a test was conducted and was not significant at either the 5 percent or 10 percent level.

are no significant differences between any of the health claim ads and nutrient content treatments.[24]

Taken together, these results suggest that heart-health claims and nutrient content claims related to saturated fat and trans fat communicate roughly the same health message to consumers, with perhaps a slight edge apparent for the direct heart-health claims. There is no evidence that the effects of nutrient content and explicit health claims are additive, and certainly the two claims do not interact synergistically to produce an effect that is greater than the sum of the parts. The results also suggest that respondents interpret the "simple" and "substitution" language in similar fashion.

Finally, adding a calorie disclosure to the Nutrient Content Simple ad has no impact on the mean healthiness rating. The Calorie Disclosure ad and the Nutrient Content Simple ad record identical scores of 4.91. We cannot determine from these results alone, however, whether respondents did not view 120 calories per serving as a cause for concern, did not make the link between possible weight gain and heart health, or possibly did not even notice the disclosure.

Figure 15 reports the results for the five Sunrise Spread treatments. As a group, the scores are slightly lower than the Sunflower Fields ratings, which suggests that respondents viewed the spread as a less heart-healthy product than the cooking oil. Still, the lowest rating–4.26 for the Tombstone Control–is above the midpoint rating of "neither bad nor good for the heart." From there, the score increases significantly to 4.99 for the Nutrient Content Simple ad (P=.001). The Health Claim Simple treatment records a mean rating that is insignificantly above the Nutrient Content Simple score (P=.31), but significantly above the Tombstone Control (P<.001).

Again, disclosing calorie information has no significant impact. There is virtually no difference between the healthiness rating for the Nutrient Content Simple ad (4.99) and the Calorie Disclosure ad (5.03). Although disclosing total fat rather than calories at least moves the mean score in the intended downward direction, from 4.99 to 4.79, this difference is not significant.

These results generally confirm the conclusions drawn from the Sunflower Fields testing. Again, the evidence shows that adding explicit information on heart health to a nutrient content claim has only a modest and insignificant positive impact on perceptions of heart-healthiness. Adding a calorie disclosure (or, for this product, a total fat disclosure) to the nutrient content claim also fails to change heart-health perceptions significantly. Finally, as explained earlier, we cannot conclude from any of these results that the nutrient content or health claims were deceptive, since respondents brought with them a prior belief that products such as those advertised were healthy for the heart when added to the diet.

_____

[24]The Health Claim Control score is significantly higher than the Nutrient Content Substitution ad score (P=.02).

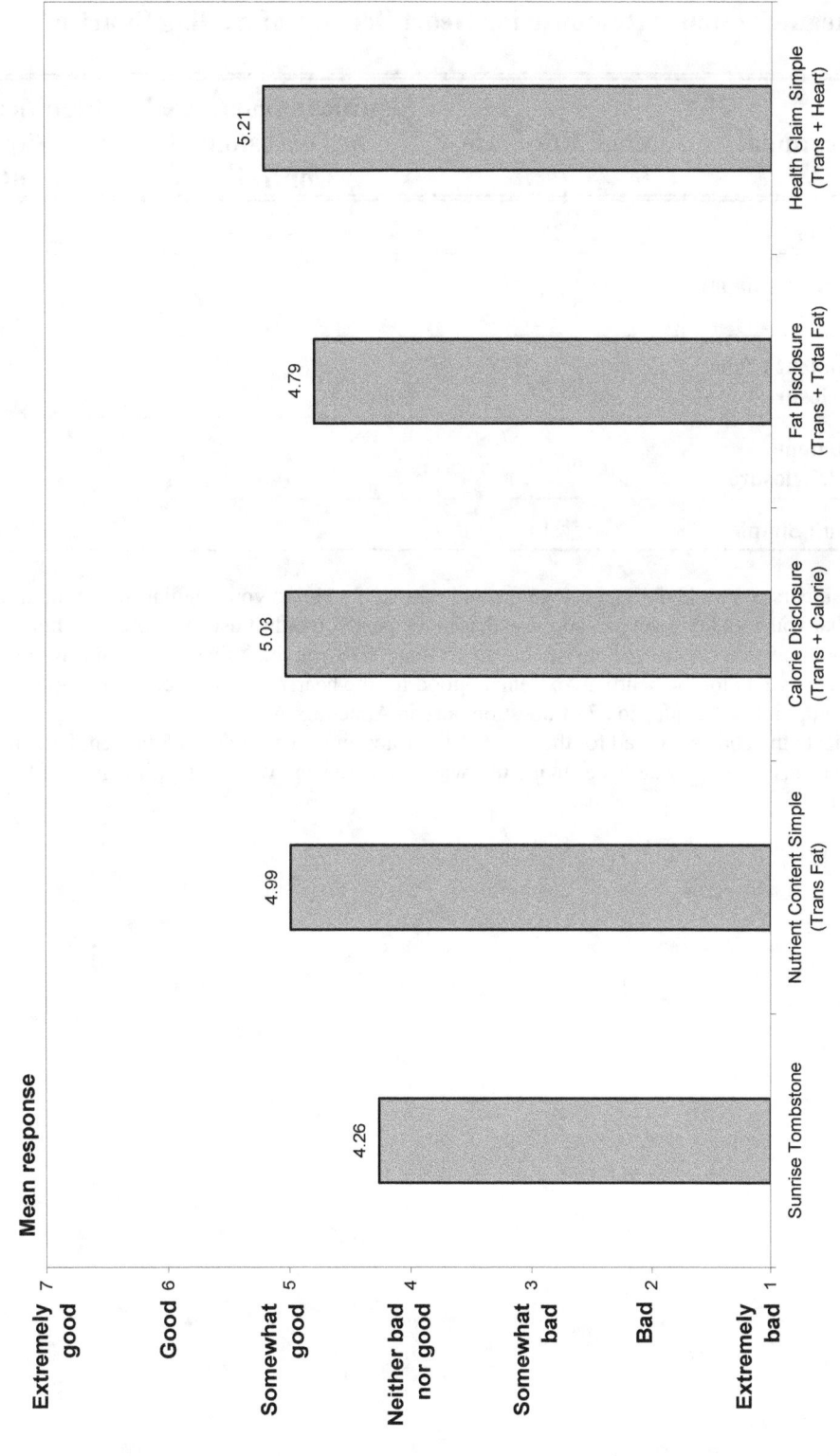

Figure 15
Sunrise Spread
Heart-Health Effect of Adding to Diet

33

Table 3 Mean Consumer Response for Heart Benefits of Adding Sunrise Spread to Diet[1]

Ad Treatment	Mean Response	Significant compared to Tombstone Control[2]	Significant compared to Simple Nutrient Content Claim[2]
Tombstone Control	4.26	---	
Nutrient Content Claim: Simple	4.99	**	---
Nutrient Content Claim: Calorie Disclosure	5.03	**	No
Nutrient Content Claim: Fat Disclosure	4.79	**	No
Health Claim: Simple	5.21	**	No

Notes. [1] Consumers were asked "Suppose you added Sunrise Spread to your regular diet without making any other changes in what you eat. For example, suppose that in the past you didn't use any spread or butter on your toast or sandwiches, but now you stat using Sunrise Spread on them. Do you think that adding Sunrise Spread to your diet would be extremely bad for the heart, ..., extremely good for the heart?" Consumers were shown a card with seven choices with endpoints. See question 7 of questionnaire in Appendix A.
[2] Dashes indicate the comparison ad for the test. ** indicates significance at the 5 percent level in a simple difference-in-means t-test. *No* indicates that a test was conducted and was not significant at either the 5 percent or 10 percent level.

2. Heart Healthiness of Substituting Tested Product for Butter or Margarine

The next question shifted the research focus to dietary substitution and asked respondents to use the same seven-point rating scale to rate the heart healthiness of using Sunflower Fields oil (Sunrise Spread) instead of butter in cooking. Since these products would in fact be better for the heart if used as replacements for worse products, rather than as dietary additions, the mean heart-healthiness scores should rise above those for the previous question if respondents are even partially aware of the nutrition issues involved. The results are reported in Figures 16 and 17.

As shown in Figure 16, which also reports the results for the prior dietary addition question from Figure 14, the new responses for Sunflower Fields are indeed uniformly higher by an amount that ranges from about .30 to .60 points. The mean response for all the dietary substitution treatments is 5.58 vs 5.05 for the "simple" treatments. This difference is highly significant (P<.001). The pattern of scores across test cells is very similar in the two graphs, with the Tombstone Control rating below that of the other test cells, and generally by a statistically significant amount.[25] As a group, the scores for three health claim ads are above the nutrient content scores, and one of these differences is statistically significant. The rating for the Health Claim Substitution treatment is significantly higher than the mean for the Nutrient Content Substitution Simple ad (P=.009).

Figure 17 illustrates that similar results hold for the Sunrise Spread dietary substitution treatments. We observe the same fairly uniform upward shift in the substitution ratings, with the overall mean increasing .27 points to 5.13 (P<.001). The Tombstone Control mean score is significantly lower than the scores for the other ads. The mean score for the one ad that includes a health claim is above the score for the corresponding nutrient content ad, although the difference is not significant. The Fat Disclosure (but not the Calorie Disclosure) appears to have had the desired effect. The mean score for the Fat Disclosure ad is significantly below the score for the Nutrient Content rating using a one-tail test (P=.052).

Overall, the results for the dietary addition and substitution questions indicate that, when asked directly, respondents on average understand that the tested products are healthier for the heart when substituted for a less healthy alternative than when added to the diet. The high mean scores for the dietary addition question suggest, however, that respondents nonetheless underestimate or do not understand the adverse impact that additional consumption of these products could have on weight gain and heart health.

---

[25]   Only the Nutrient Content Substitution claim fails statistical significance using a one-tail test.

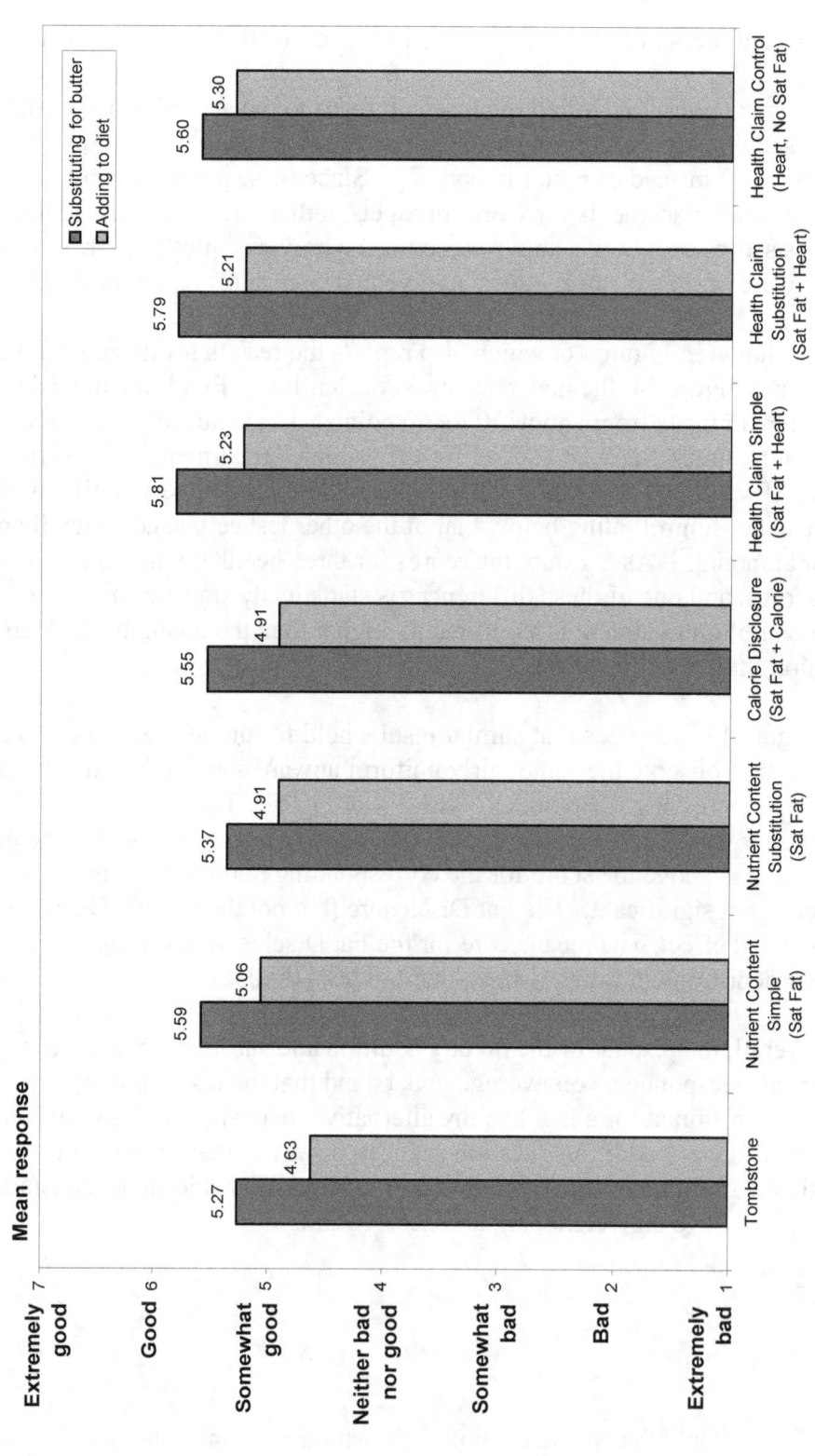

Figure 16
Sunflower Fields
Heart-Health Effect of Substituting for Butter

36

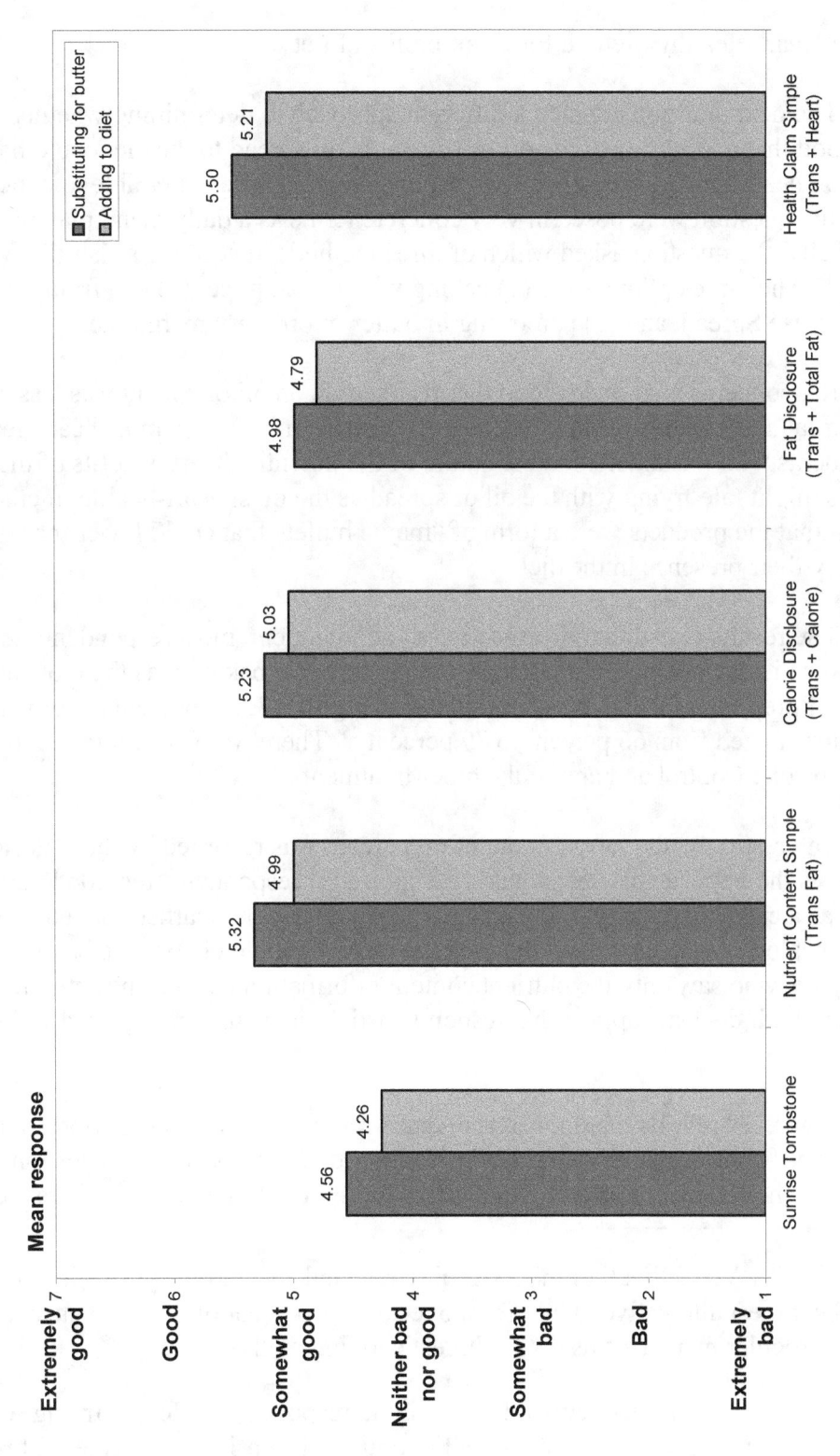

Figure 17
Sunrise Spread
Heart-Health Effect of Substituting for Butter

37

3. Most Heart-Healthy Method for Cooking Fish Filet

The next question adopted a different approach to determining whether respondents understood that adding a cooking oil or vegetable oil spread to the diet could have a negative impact on heart health. We hoped that respondents might be better able to conceptualize this issue if the question were posed in very concrete terms as a daily menu planning decision. Specifically, the question asked which of three methods of cooking a fish filet was healthiest for the heart. The three options were (1) baking with lemon juice; (2) pan frying in Sunflower Fields oil or Sunrise Spread; and (3) pan frying in butter or ordinary margarine.

Respondents who understood that frying with an oil or spread was less heart-healthy than avoiding fat altogether would rate baking with lemon juice as the most heart-healthy alternative. Respondents who misunderstood the nature of the potential heart benefits of the advertised products might rate frying with the oil or spread as the most heart-healthy method, perhaps thinking that the products were a form of "magic bullet" that could lower the risk of heart disease simply by their presence in the diet.

The results reveal that, irrespective of ad treatment, most respondents seeing the Sunflower Fields cooking oil treatments understood that baking was the most heart-healthy method of preparing the fish filet. As shown in Figure 18, the percentage of respondents selecting this option ranged from 66 percent to 79 percent.[26] There were no significant differences between the Tombstone Control and any of the other treatments.

Interestingly, the lowest score of 66 percent was recorded by the Calorie Disclosure. This outcome is the opposite of what would be expected if respondents regarded 120 calories per serving as a cause for concern. Presumably, consumers who learned that the cooking oil was higher in calories than they thought would be *more* likely to choose the baking option than would respondents who saw only the nutrient content information concerning saturated fat. Accordingly, it does not appear that respondents in this treatment regarded 120 calories as a high number.

Figure 19 reveals that most respondents seeing the five Sunrise Spread ads also chose baking over frying with either Sunrise Spread or butter. These percentages ranged from 65 percent for the Health Claim ad to 80 percent for the Fat Disclosure.[27] There were no statistically

---

[26] Virtually all of the remaining respondents chose frying with Sunflower Fields oil as the healthiest alternative. Only from one-to-four percent of respondents chose frying with butter or regular margarine as the healthiest cooking method.

[27] Again, very few of the remaining respondents selected frying with butter or regular margarine as the most heart-healthy option. From 19 to 38 percent of respondents rated frying with Sunrise Spread as the most heart-healthy option.

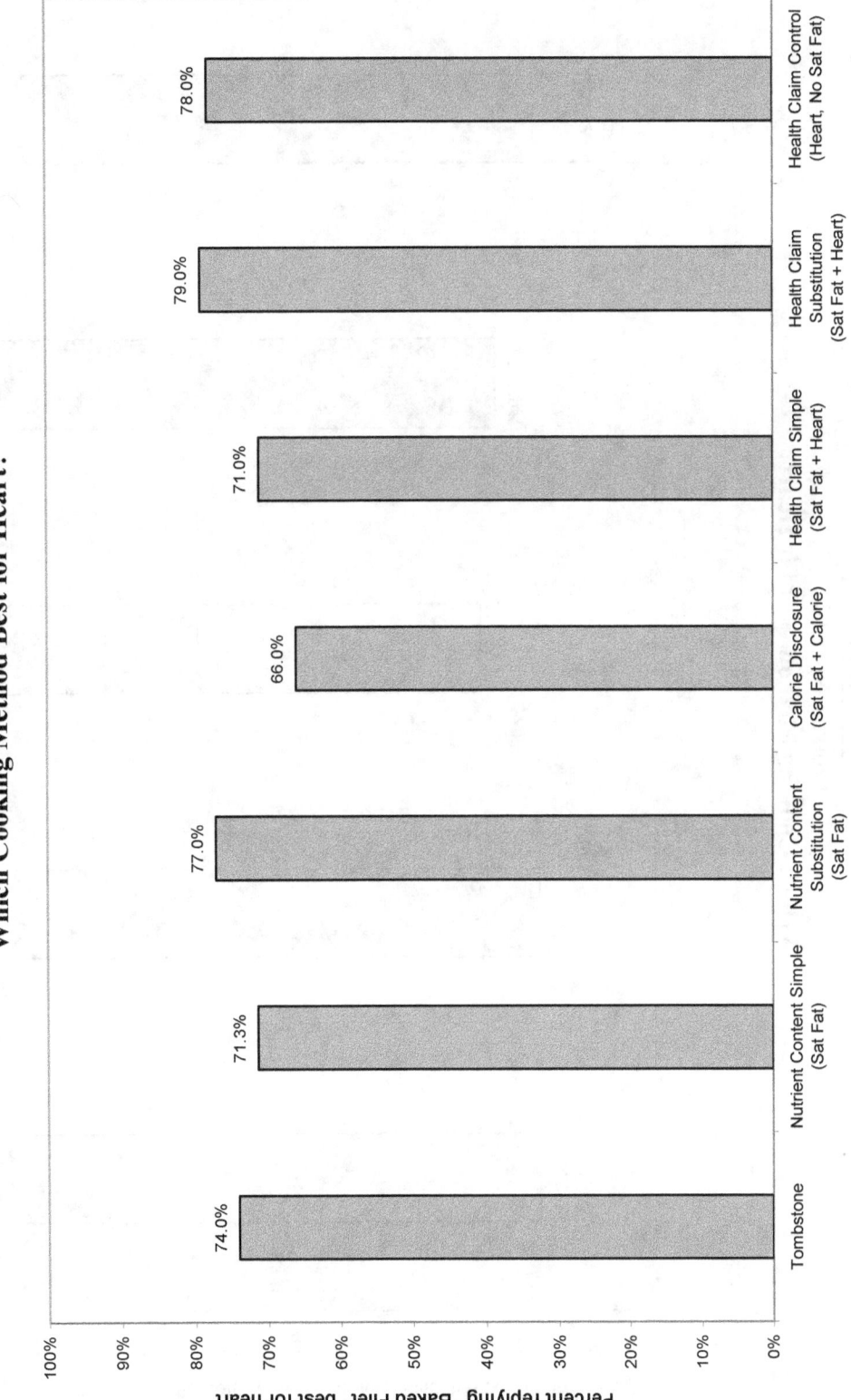

Figure 18
Sunflower Fields
Which Cooking Method Best for Heart?

39

Figure 19
Sunrise Spread
Which Cooking Method Best for Heart?

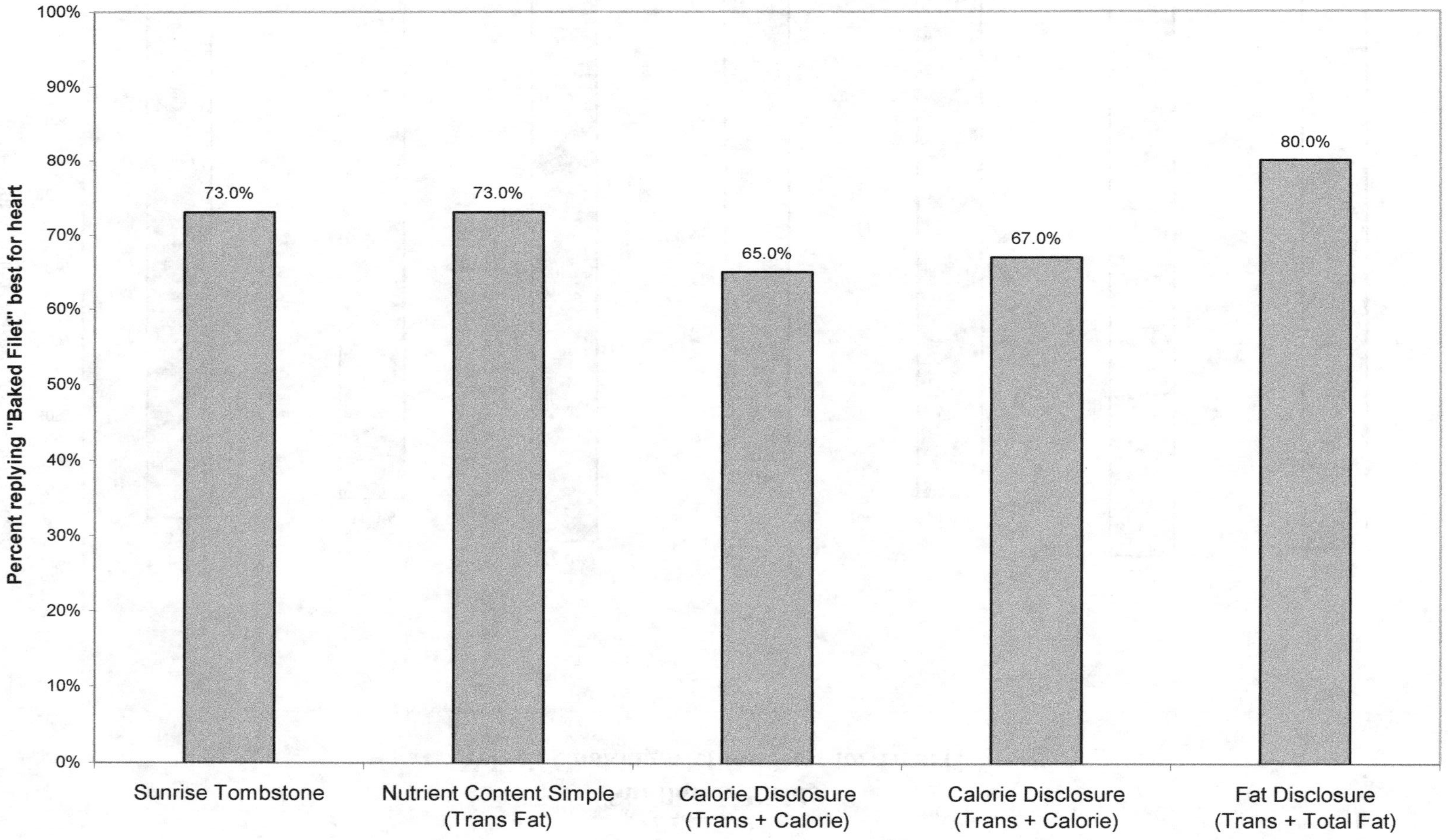

Percent replying "Baked Filet" best for heart

- Sunrise Tombstone: 73.0%
- Nutrient Content Simple (Trans Fat): 73.0%
- Calorie Disclosure (Trans + Calorie): 65.0%
- Calorie Disclosure (Trans + Calorie): 67.0%
- Fat Disclosure (Trans + Total Fat): 80.0%

40

significant differences between the scores of any of the ads that did not disclose total fat content. Although the Fat Disclosure score of 80 percent was not significantly higher than the Nutrient Content or Tombstone Control ratings, it was the highest recorded and was significantly higher than the score of 67 percent for the Calorie Disclosure ad (P=.04). This suggests that respondents were more concerned by the amount of total fat in Sunrise Spread (10 grams per serving) than by the caloric content *per se* (90 per serving).

In sum, these results suggest that most respondents understand that the advertised products do not possess pharmaceutical-like powers that offset any undesirable effects attributable to their fat content. The large majority of respondents view avoiding an oil or spread altogether as more heart healthy than using the advertised products in cooking. The results do not reveal, however, any specific information about respondents' understanding of the fat and calorie profiles of the tested products, or the implications of this fat and calorie content for weight gain. These issues are explored below.

4. Effect of Regular Use of Sunrise Spread on Weight Loss

As discussed, our initial analysis of the Sunflower Fields results suggested that consumers may have interpreted the opening questions on heart health very narrowly and were not prompted to consider any indirect effects regular use of the product might have on heart health through the mechanism of weight gain. The Sunrise Spread respondents were therefore asked the following question that focused directly on the issue of weight:

> Suppose someone you know has been using Sunrise Spread, and now decides to go on a diet to lose weight. Also suppose this person continues to use Sunrise Spread on a regular basis. Do you think that using Sunrise Spread on a regular basis would be: extremely bad for losing weight, bad for losing weight, somewhat bad for losing weight, neither good nor bad for losing weight, somewhat good for losing weight, good for losing weight, or extremely good for losing weight.

This question provides the first clear test of whether the nutrient content and health claim information lowers respondents' perceptions of the calorie or fat content of Sunrise Spread. The appropriateness of using this product as part of a diet to lose weight depends strictly on its calorie content, which in turn is related to total fat content–not the composition of that fat If consumers understand this, the average responses for the treatment groups should not be significantly higher than the mean response for the Tombstone Control ad. If, however, respondents form a more favorable opinion of Sunrise Spread as a diet aid after seeing the Nutrient Content ad or Health Claim ad, this evidence would indicate that the positive messages about trans fatty acid content or heart health were causing some consumers to infer incorrectly that the product was lower in calories and better suited for a weight loss program than ordinary spreads.

Figure 20 and Table 4 report the results for the diet question. All of the mean ratings, including the Calorie Disclosure and Fat Disclosure, are above the midpoint rating of 4.0 ("Neither good nor bad" for losing weight), which indicates that respondents on average overestimated the appropriateness of using the spread in a weight program. The Nutrient Content rating of 4.90 is significantly above the Tombstone Control rating of 4.04 (P<.001), which provides evidence of a halo effect from the "no trans fatty acids" claim. The additional heart-health information in the Health Claim ad does not, however, magnify this effect. The Health Claim mean is virtually identical to the Nutrient Content mean.

The Calorie Disclosure, which registers the *highest* mean response (5.18), clearly failed to perform its intended task. Although the Fat Disclosure score is significantly below the score for the Nutrient Content ad, the Fat Disclosure mean rating is still significantly above the Tombstone Control rating, which means that the disclosure of total fat did not eliminate the halo effect from the nutrient content information in the Fat Disclosure ad.

5. Calories Compared to Butter

The next two questions focused directly on the caloric content of the advertised products. Respondents were first asked the following comparative question:

Based on what the ad says or suggests, or anything else you may know or believe, would you say that one tablespoon of Sunflower Fields (Sunrise Spread) is much higher in calories than one tablespoon of butter, somewhat higher in calories than butter, about equal in calories to butter, somewhat lower in calories than butter, or much lower in calories than butter?

a. Sunflower Fields

For Sunflower Fields oil, the correct answer is "somewhat higher in calories than butter," since cooking oils are entirely fat and contain 120 calories per 14-gram serving (one tablespoon), whereas butter and stick margarine have about 11 grams of fat per serving, which corresponds to 100 calories. It was not expected, however, that many consumers would be aware of this arguably esoteric fact. Rather, the primary objectives of the question were to determine (1) whether respondents seriously underestimated the calories in Sunflower Fields relative to butter, (2)

42

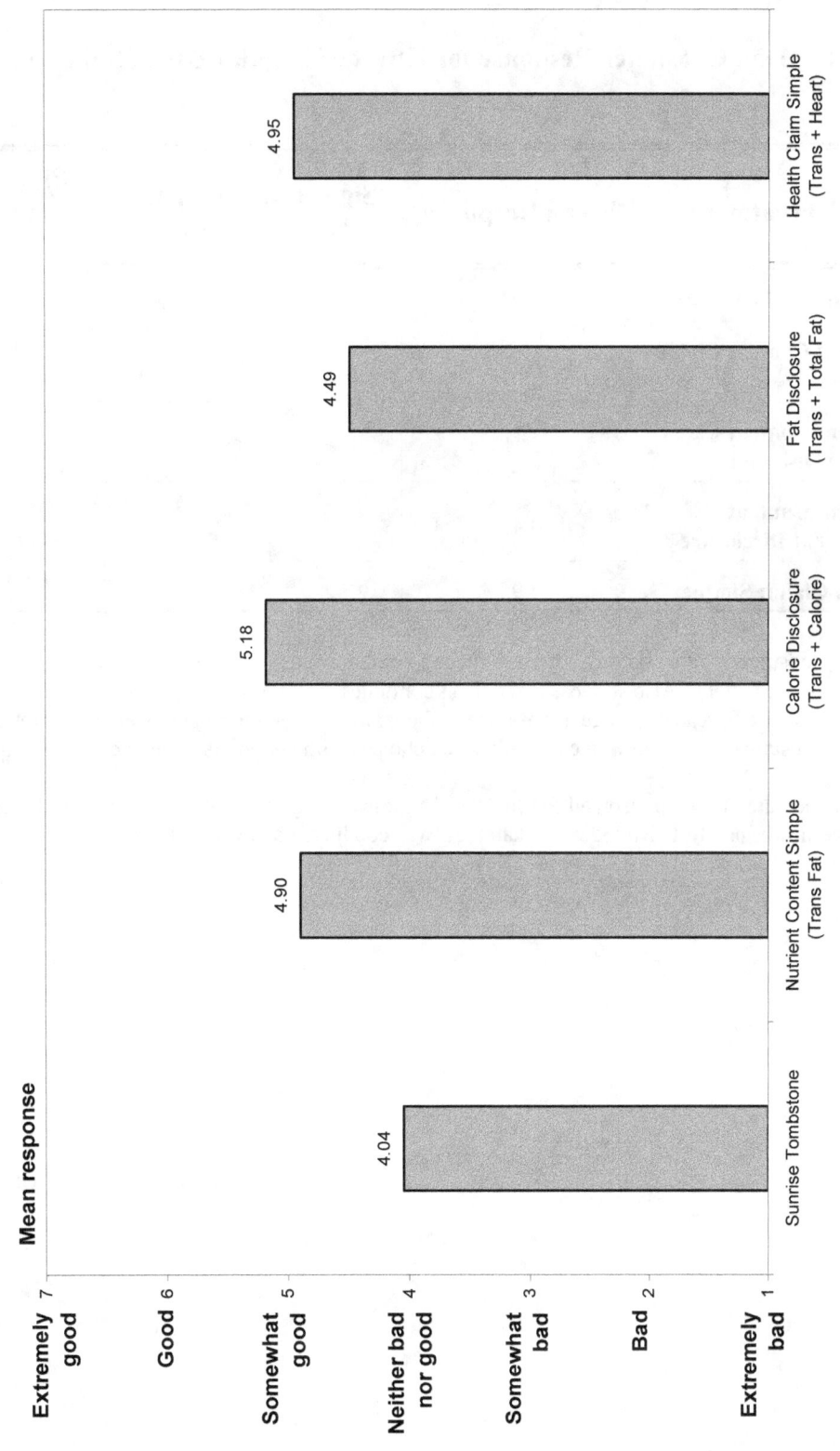

Figure 20
Sunrise Spread
How Good is Reular Use for Losing Weight

43

Table 4 Mean Consumer Response for Effect of Regular Use of Sunrise Spread on Weight Loss[1]

Ad Treatment	Mean Response	Significant compared to Tombstone Control[2]	Significant compared to Simple Nutrient Content Claim[2]
Tombstone Control	4.04	---	
Nutrient Content Claim: Simple	4.90	**	---
Nutrient Content Claim: Calorie Disclosure	5.18	**	No
Nutrient Content Claim: Fat Disclosure	4.49	**	**
Health Claim: Simple	4.95	**	No

Notes. [1] Consumers were asked "Suppose someone you know has been using Sunrise Spread, and now decides to go on a diet to lose weight. Also suppose this person continues to use Sunrise Spread on a regular basis. Do you think that using Sunrise Spread on a regular basis would be: extremely bad for losing weight...extremely good for losing weight? Consumers were shown a card with seven choices with endpoints. See question 9 of questionnaire in Appendix
[2] Dashes indicate the comparison ad for the test. ** indicates significance at the 5 percent level in a simple difference-in-means t-test. *No* indicates that a test was conducted and was not significant.

whether the nutrient content and health claims lowered the average ratings relative to the ratings for the Tombstone Control, and if so, (3) whether a calorie disclosure or total fat disclosure would counteract this halo effect.

Figure 21 presents the mean ratings for the seven Sunflower Fields treatment groups. There are no statistically significant differences among test groups, indicating that the various claims and the disclosure of calories-per-serving had no overall impact on respondents' impressions of the relative caloric content of cooking oil and butter. The absolute level of all the scores, however, indicates clearly that respondents on average underestimated the number of calories in cooking oil relative to butter. These scores, which vary narrowly from 1.71 to 1.89, are all below "Somewhat lower than butter." Virtually no respondents in any of the test groups gave the technically correct answer of "somewhat higher in calories." A substantial percentage of respondents gave the least correct rating of "much lower in calories." This proportion ranged from 32 percent (Tombstone Control) to 49 percent (Health Claim Substitution).

The failure of the Calorie Disclosure to affect respondents' average perceptions of the relative calorie content of the cooking oil suggests that consumers do not regard 120 calories per serving as a high number, even when the serving size is only one tablespoon. This in turn indicates that the respondents in this test cell apparently believed mistakenly that butter contains considerably more than 120 calories per serving. (The poor performance of this disclosure cannot be attributed to a failure of respondents to notice it. As is discussed below, a substantial number of respondents apparently did see and remember the calorie information in the ad.)

a. Sunrise Spread

For Sunrise Spread, which contains 90 calories per serving, the correct answer could be either "about equal in calories to butter" or perhaps "somewhat lower in calories than butter." As shown in Figure 22, the average ratings for the five test ads clustered around "somewhat lower in calories than butter." There is evidence of a halo effect for the Nutrient Content ad, which registers a score significantly below the Tombstone Control (P=.019).

Although the Health Claim mean is also significantly below the Tombstone Control (P=.043), the difference between the Nutrient Content and Health Claim scores is not statistically significant. Thus, only the nutrient content information concerning trans fatty acids contributes to the observed halo effect. The difference between the Nutrient Content and Tombstone mean ratings loses statistical significance when either the Calorie or Fat disclosure is included in the ad (although the ratings for the Calorie and Fat disclosure ads are not significantly above the Nutrient Content and Health Claim ad ratings).

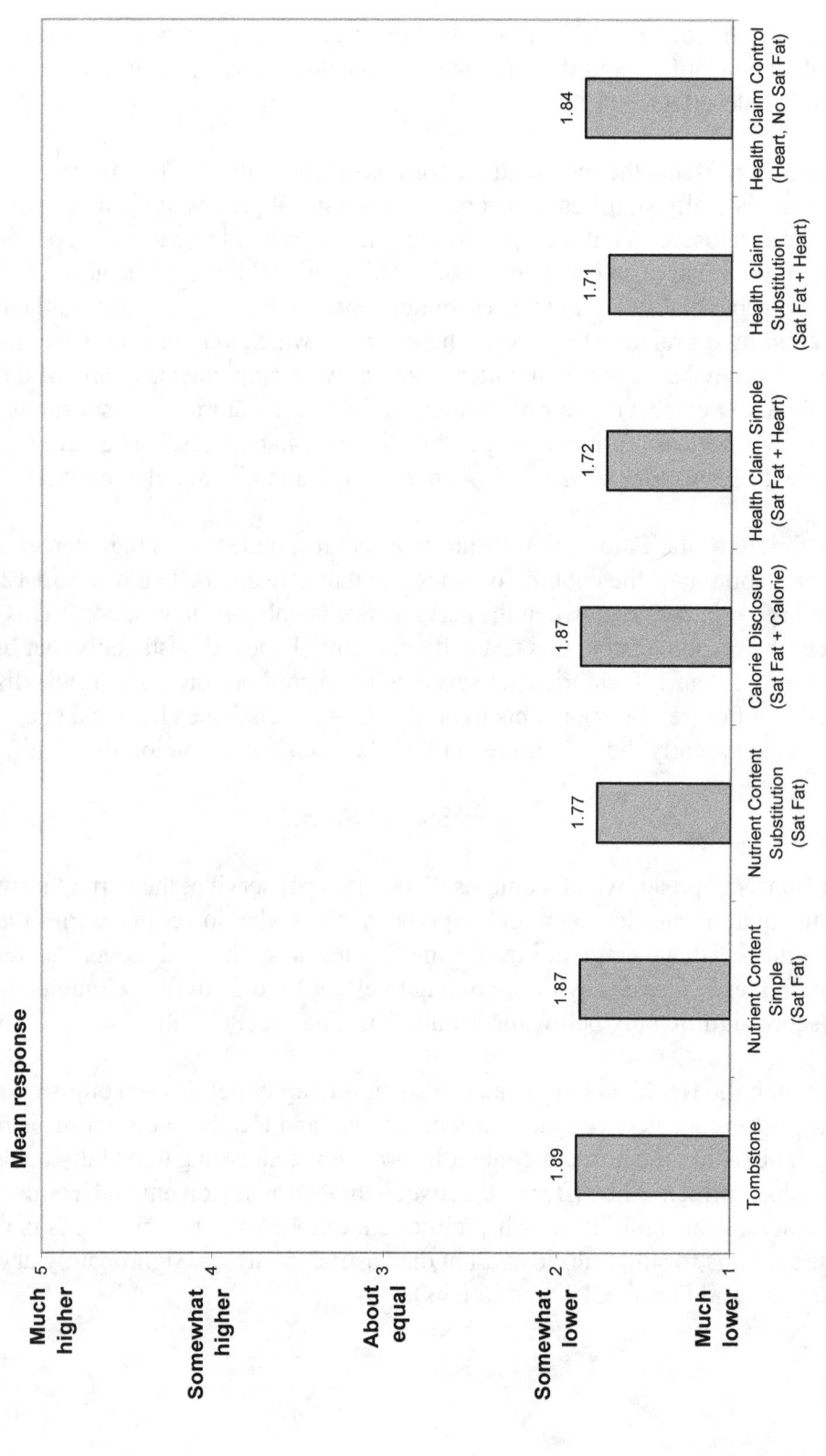

Figure 21
Sunflower Fields
Calories Compared to Butter*

* No significant differences between treatment cell means.

46

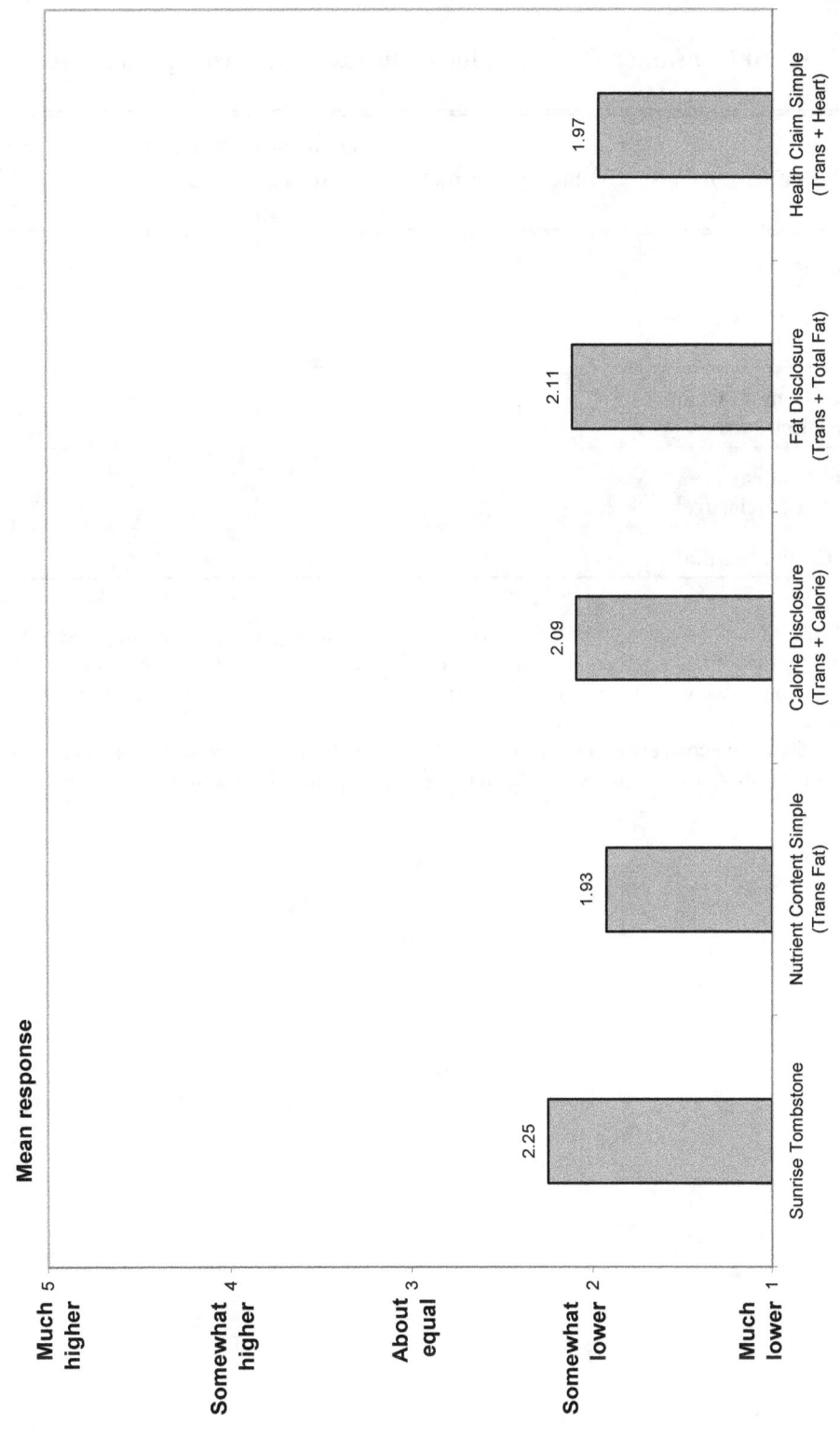

Figure 22
Sunrise Spread
Calories Compared to Butter

47

Table 5 Mean Consumer Response for Calories in Sunrise Spread Compared to Butter[1]

Ad Treatment	Mean Response	Significant compared to Tombstone Control[2]	Significant compared to Simple Nutrient Content Claim[2]
Tombstone Control	2.25	---	
Nutrient Content Claim: Simple	1.93	**	---
Nutrient Content Claim: Calorie Disclosure	2.09	No	No
Nutrient Content Claim: Fat Disclosure	2.11	No	No
Health Claim: Simple	1.97	**	No

Notes. [1] Consumers were asked "Based on what the ad says or suggests, or anything else you may know or believe, would you say that one tablespoon of Sunrise Spread is much higher...much lower in calories than one tablespoon of butter? Consumers were shown a card with seven choices with endpoints. See question 10 of questionnaire in Appendix A.
[2] Dashes indicate the comparison ad for the test. ** indicates significance at the 5 percent level in a simple difference-in-means t-test. *No* indicates that a test was conducted and was not significant.

The proportion of respondents that gave the least correct answer of "much lower in calories than butter" was lower for the Sunrise Spread ads than for the Sunflower Field ads. The Sunrise Spread proportions ranged from 22 percent for the Tombstone Control to 39 percent for the Nutrient Content ad.[28]

In comparison to the Sunflower Fields ratings, these results indicate that consumers have a better understanding of the number of calories in Sunrise Spread relative to butter, although the evidence indicates a halo effect from the no-trans-fatty-acids claim. This effect can be offset by disclosing either the quantity of calories or total fat per serving in the ad.

6. Absolute Number of Calories

Finally, respondents were asked directly to estimate the absolute number of calories in a serving of Sunflower Fields oil or Sunrise Spread. Five ranges were provided: 0-50, 51-100, 101-150, 151-200, and more than 200. (In this and most other questions, the order in which the options were presented was rotated to avoid any order bias.)

a. Sunflower Fields Oil

Since all cooking oils contain 120 calories per tablespoon, the correct answer for the Sunflower Fields ads would be the third category–101-150 calories. Figure 23 reveals that, with the exception of the Calorie Disclosure test group, all of the means are below the second category of 51-100 calories. Evidence for a halo effect is very limited. Only the mean for the Nutrient Content Substitution ad is significantly lower than that of the Tombstone Control.[29]

The Calorie Disclosure mean of 2.36 is significantly higher than any of the other means, including the Tombstone Control, although below the value of 3.0 that would have been achieved had all of the respondents in this group seen and remembered the disclosure of 120 calories per tablespoon. The distribution of scores across response categories reveals that 52 percent

---

[28] This difference is statistically significant (P=.022). For the Health Claim ad, the proportion of respondents answering "much lower in calories than butter" was 34 percent, which is not significantly higher than the Tombstone Control proportion (P=.12).

[29] There is no *a priori* reason why the Nutrient Control Substitution claim should have lowered respondents' perception of caloric content more than did the other treatments. This isolated result therefore should not be accorded a great deal of importance given that there were multiple opportunities for a significant difference to emerge by chance in this series of tests.

Figure 23
Sunflower Fields
Number of Calories per Tablespoon

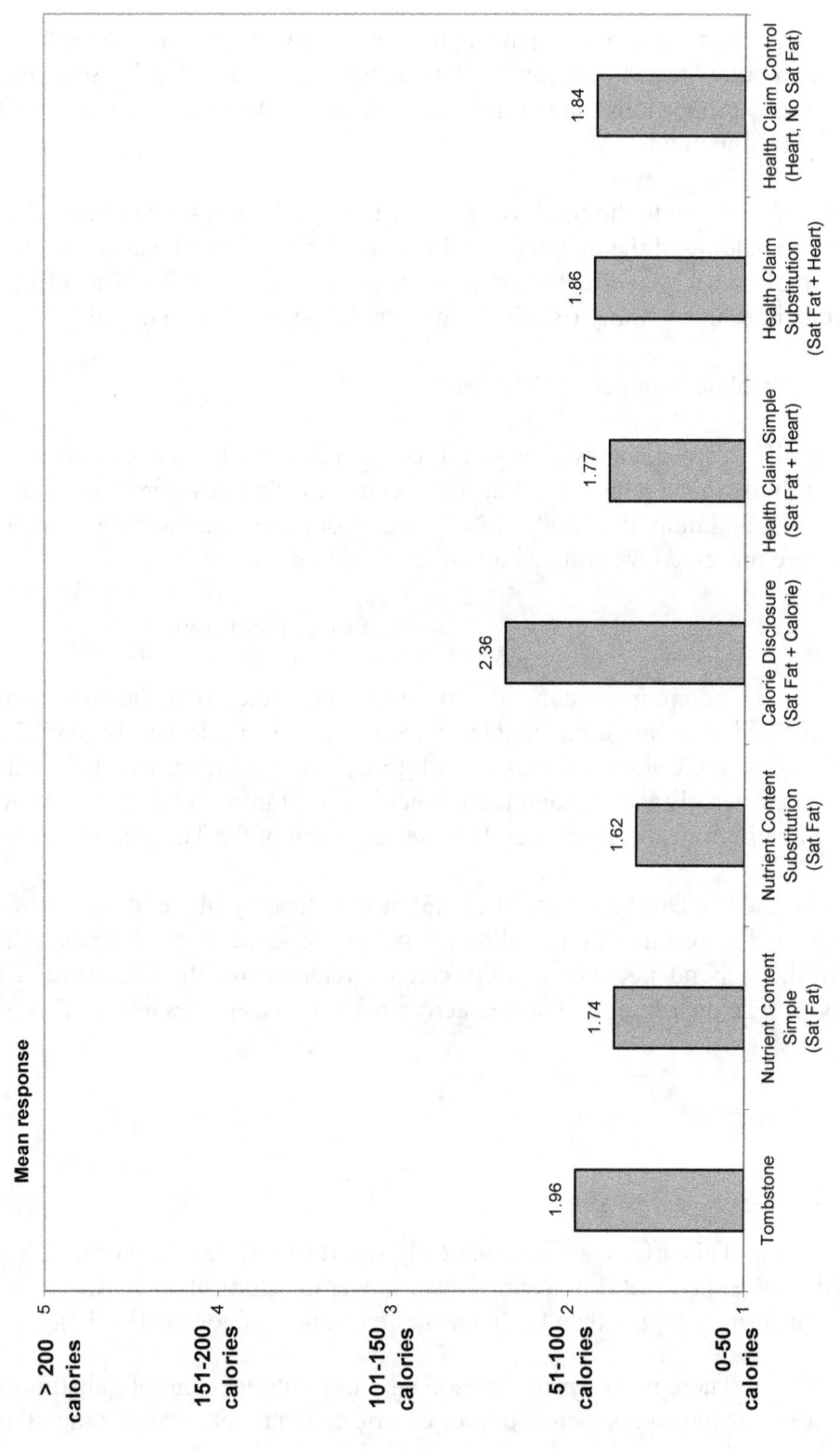

Table 6 Mean Consumer Response for Number of Calories in One Tablespoon of Sunflower Fields Oil[1]

Ad Treatment	Mean Response	Significant compared to Tombstone Control[2]	Significant compared to Simple Nutrient Content Claim[2]
Tombstone Control	1.96	---	
Nutrient Content Claim: Simple	1.74	No	---
Nutrient Content Claim: Substitution	1.62	**	No
Nutrient Content Claim: Calorie Disclosure	2.36	**	**
Health Claim: Simple	1.77	No	No
Health Claim: Substitution	1.66	No	No
Health Claim: Control	1.84	No	No

Notes. [1] Consumers were asked "Based on what the ad says or suggests, or anything else you may know or believe, about how many calories are in one tablespoon of Sunflower Fields? Consumers were shown a card with five choices with endpoints. See question 12 of questionnaire in appendix.

[2] Dashes indicate the comparison ad for the test. ** indicates significance at the 5 percent level in a simple difference-in-means t-test. *No* indicates that a test was conducted and was not significant.

of these respondents selected the correct category. The comparable figures for the other test conditions range from five to 15 percent, which indicates that on net approximately two-fifths of the respondents noticed and recalled the calorie information in the ad.

In sum, the results from this question provide further evidence that consumers underestimate the calorie density of cooking oil. The results also suggest that disclosing calories-per-serving can provide a partial remedy for any enhancement of this misunderstanding caused by the saturated fat nutrient content claim.[30] The lack of a clear halo effect in the various health claim and nutrient content claim treatments, however, indicates that there may not be any deceptive inferences in these ads that would justify such a disclosure.

b. Sunrise Spread

Spreads in stick form, such as Sunrise Spread, generally contain 90 calories per tablespoon. The correct answer to the calorie question therefore was the second category–51-100 calories. The results, shown in Figure 24, contrast sharply with the Sunflower Fields outcome. Respondents seeing the first three ads on average very slightly *over*estimated the number of calories in Sunrise Spread. The results reveal no evidence of a halo effect; neither the Health Claim nor the Nutrient Content mean is significantly below the Tombstone Control average.

Surprisingly, disclosing either calories or total fat lowers the average score to below the correct value of 51-100 calories, although the only significant differences (using a one-tail test) are between these means and the Tombstone Control mean (P=.07 for the Calorie Disclosure; P=.10 for the Fat Disclosure.) In any event, these disclosures clearly had a very modest impact, and arguably did not on net improve consumer understanding of the caloric content of the product.

7. Purchase Interest

As is customary in consumer research of this type, a question was included to measure the overall purchase appeal of the test products. Such a question helps place the research issues in better perspective by probing how important consumers considered the information presented in the ads. If, for example, the purchase interest scores given by respondents seeing the Tombstone

---

[30] Disclosing calories might not be of any practical value, however, given the poor and even perverse performance of the Calorie Disclosure in the previous questions. It is not clear that consumers would appreciate the health implications of consuming a product with as many as 120 calories per tablespoon even if they learned how many calories were in the product.

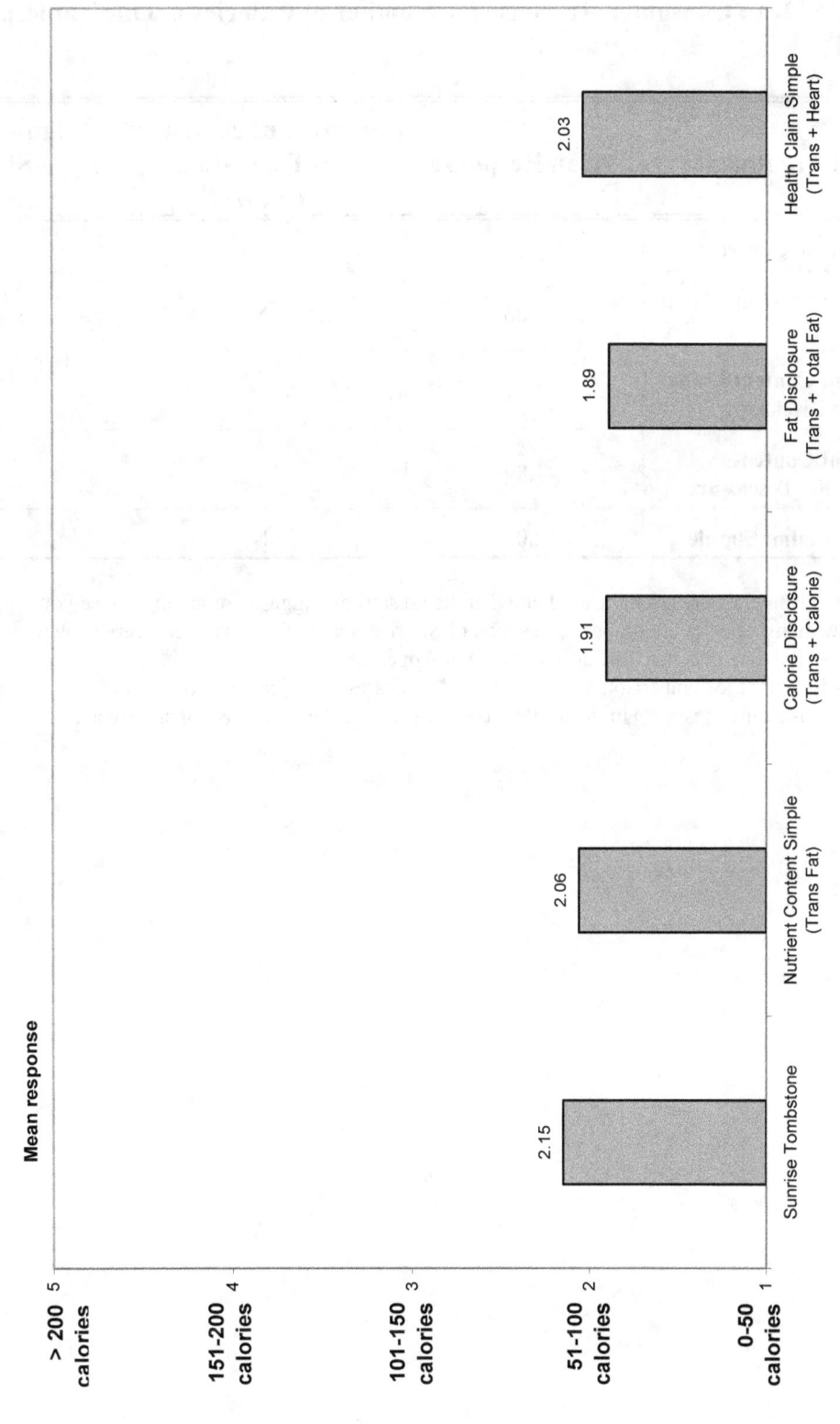

Figure 24
Sunrise Spread
Number of Calories per Tablespoon

53

Table 7   Mean Consumer Response for Number of Calories in One Tablespoon of Sunrise Spread[1]

Ad Treatment	Mean Response	Significant compared to Tombstone Control[2]	Significant compared to Simple Nutrient Content Claim[2]
Tombstone Control	2.15	---	
Nutrient Content Claim: Simple	2.06	No	---
Nutrient Content Claim: Calorie Disclosure	1.91	*	No
Nutrient Content Claim: Fat Disclosure	1.89	*	No
Health Claim: Simple	2.03	No	No

Notes. [1] Consumers were asked "Based on what the ad says or suggests, or anything else you may know or believe, about how many calories are on one tablespoon of Sunrise Spread?" Consumers were shown a card with five choices with endpoints. See question 7 of questionnaire in Appendix A.
[2] Dashes indicate the comparison ad for the test. * indicates significance at the 10 percent level in a simple difference-in-means t-test. *No* indicates that a test was conducted and was not significant.

Control ad (which provided no specific information about the product) were as high as those for the treatment groups, we could conclude that consumers were not very interested in the nutrient content and health claim information that was provided.

The specific question asked was: "How interested would you be in buying the product? There were five response categories, which ranged from "Not at all interested" to "Extremely interested." Figures 25 and 26 present the mean ratings for the Sunflower Fields oil and Sunrise Spread treatments, respectively.

Sunflower Fields oil registered moderately high purchase appeal, with the mean scores all between "Somewhat interested" and "Very interested." The overall mean is 3.31. The Tombstone Control mean is the lowest of the group, although the largest difference (between the Health Claim Control and the Tombstone Control) is not quite significant. The means for the remaining test conditions are very similar. It should be noted in particular that the disclosure of calories-per-serving had virtually no effect on purchase interest, which is yet another indication that consumers did not consider 120 calories-per-tablespoon a cause for concern. Taken as a whole, the results suggest that consumers valued the information concerning saturated fat only slightly, and did not place any additional value on the health information linking diets low in saturated fat to a reduced risk of heart disease.

Respondents were less attracted to the Sunrise Spread product. The overall mean score is 2.97, with the Tombstone Control again recording the lowest mean (2.74). Unlike the Sunflower Fields results, there is a significant increase in purchase interest over the Tombstone Control for the Nutrient Content, Health Claim, and Calorie treatments.[31] Indeed, the Calorie ad registered the highest rating of 3.18, which indicates that the disclosure failed to communicate that the product in question was calorically dense.

Neither the Health Claim nor Calorie Disclosure scores differs significantly from the Nutrient Content score, however. This outcome is consistent with prior findings that only the nutrient content information concerning trans fatty acids contributed to any halo effects that emerged. Again consistent with previous results, the Fat Disclosure outperforms the Calorie Disclosure in communicating negative information about Sunrise Spread's nutrient profile. The purchase interest score for the Fat Disclosure is significantly lower than that of the Calorie Disclosure ($P=.005$) and is not statistically distinguishable from the Tombstone Control mean.

---

[31]   The P values were .05, .03., and 001, respectively.

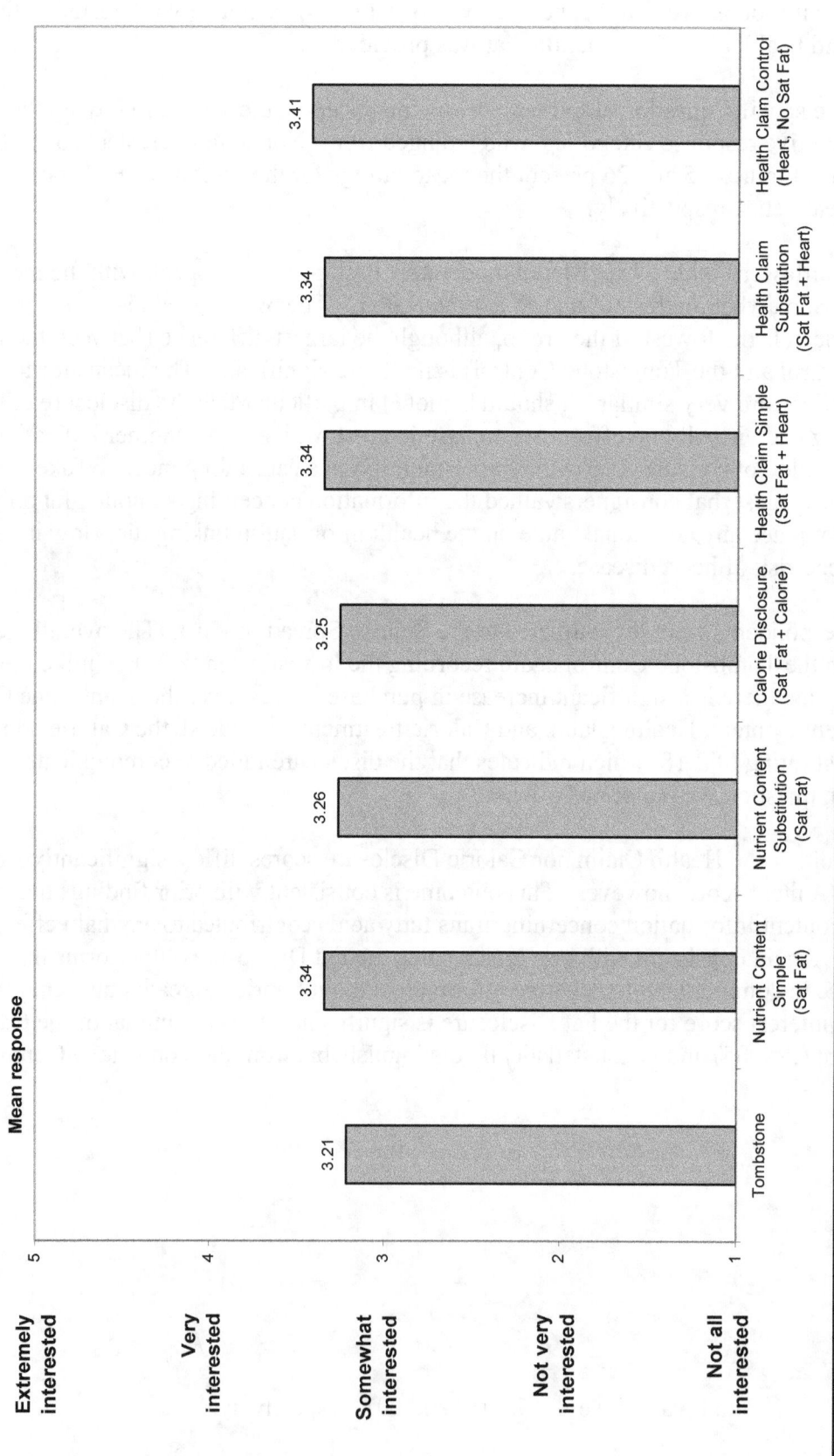

Figure 25
Sunflower Fields
Purchase Interest*

* No significant differences between treatment cell means.

56

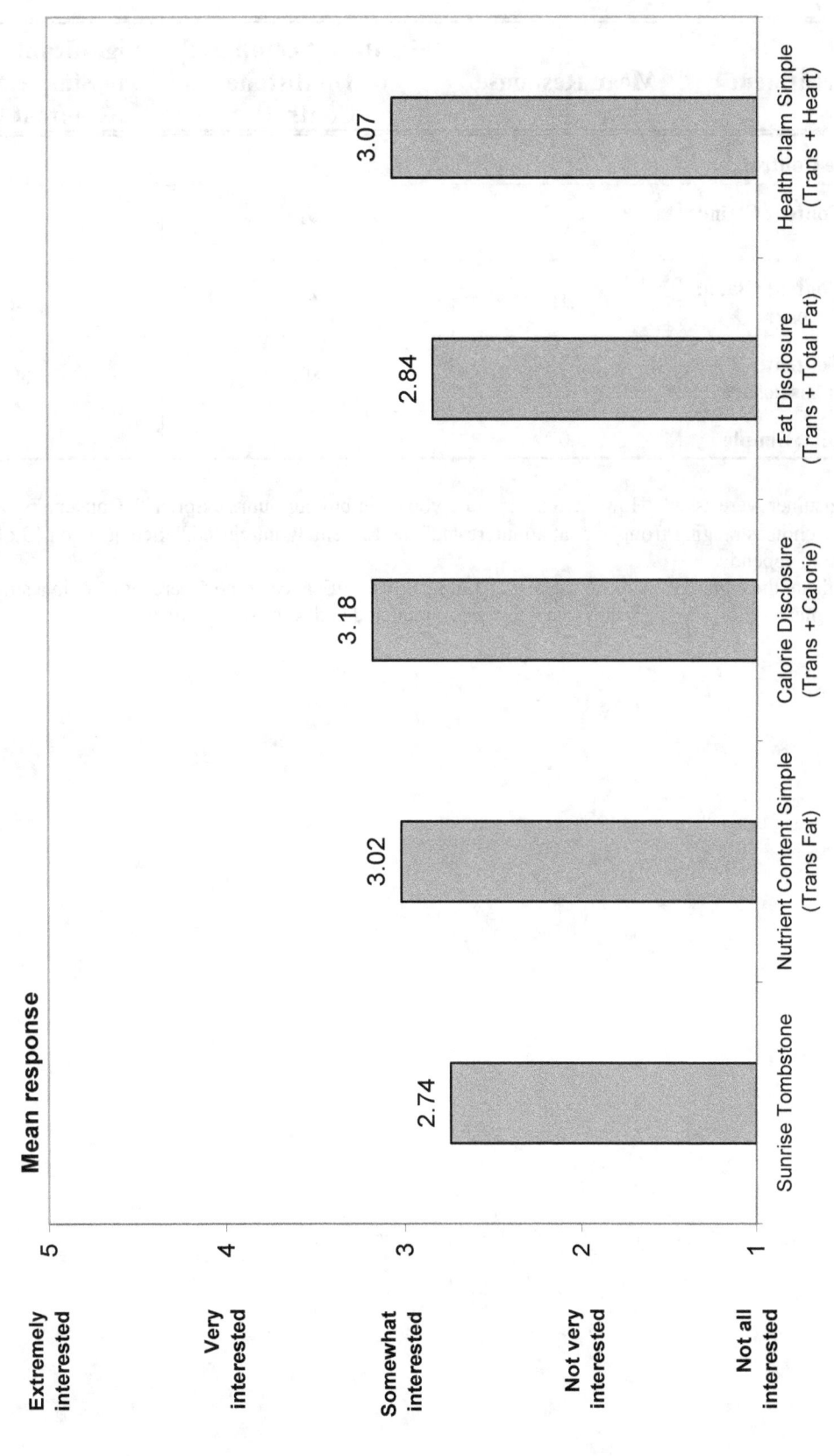

Figure 26
Sunrise Spread
Purchase interest

Mean response

57

Table 8   Mean Consumer Response for Sunrise Spread Purchase Interest[1]

Ad Treatment	Mean Response	Significant compared to Tombstone Control[2]	Significant compared to Simple Nutrient Content Claim[2]
Tombstone Control	2.74	---	
Nutrient Content Claim: Simple	3.02	**	---
Nutrient Content Claim: Calorie Disclosure	3.18	**	No
Nutrient Content Claim: Fat Disclosure	2.84	No	No
Health Claim: Simple	3.07	**	No

Notes. [1] Consumer were asked "How interested would you be in buying Sunrise Spread? Consumers were shown a card with five choices ranging from "Not at all interested" to "Extremely interested." See question 13 of questionnaire in appendix.
[2] Dashes indicate the comparison ad for the test. ** indicates significance at the 5 percent level in a simple difference-in-means t-test. *No* indicates that a test was conducted and was not significant.

8. Personal Characteristics

Our inquiry concluded with questions concerning the personal characteristics of respondents, including their education and income level, and whether or not they had been on a diet to lose weight during the last year. Data on respondent age and gender were obtained during the initial screening interviews. There were five categories for the age, income, and education variables, represented in each case by four dummy variables (with the lowest category omitted).

All else equal, we would expect more educated and higher income respondents to be better informed about nutrition issues in general, and perhaps also about the specific nutrient profile of the tested products. We would also expect respondents who had tried to lose weight recently to be more interested in and knowledgeable about the calorie and fat content of food products. The independent influence of age is more difficult to predict *a priori*. Older respondents might be more concerned about health issues and have gained more knowledge about nutrition through greater experience, but might also exhibit some reduced cognitive function.

The research used probit analysis to determine whether consumers with certain characteristics were more likely to select an answer that was unambiguously incorrect and that evidenced a degree of misunderstanding that could have significant health consequences.[32] Five of the close-ended questions were included in the analysis (with one probit regression for each question). To illustrate, for the question that asked respondents to compare the caloric content of Sunflower fields or Sunrise Spread with butter, an answer of "much lower in calories than butter" would reflect a serious misunderstanding of the caloric content of the test product.[33]

Data for all of the treatments and the two products were pooled. We used a dummy

---

[32]   We also used a second and more general approach to measuring the impact of personal characteristics. Ordered probit regressions tested whether there were any systematic relationships between the selected personal characteristics and the overall pattern of the question responses. It will be recalled that, particularly for Sunflower Fields, respondents generally chose answers that placed the nutrient profile of the test products in too favorable a light. That is, respondents on average chose response categories that were too high numerically. The ordered probit regressions would reveal whether, for example, more highly educated respondents systematically chose more correct responses. The results using this general approach did not differ substantively from the findings of the first approach discussed above, and are not reported.

[33]   For the question that asked respondents to rate on a seven-point scale how good for the heart was adding the test product to the diet with no other changes, any response of five ("Somewhat good for the heart") or higher was considered incorrect. Similarly, any answer of five or greater was considered incorrect for the question that asked how good for losing weight was adding Sunrise Spread to the diet on a regular basis. For the question that asked for the most heart-healthy method of cooking a filet of fish, any answer other than baking was considered incorrect. Finally, for the question that asked how many calories were in a serving of the test product, an answer of 0-50 calories was considered incorrect.

variable, which assumed the value of one for all of the Sunrise Spread treatments, to determine whether there were any systematic differences between the two test products in the impact of the demographic variables.[34]

Full results for the five probit equations are shown in Appendix B. These results show no significant relationship between the question responses and the variable that measured whether or not a respondent had been on a diet to lose weight during the past year. In contrast, respondents with the highest income level (greater than $75,000 per year) consistently gave fewer wrong answers.[35]

Only two of the education dummy variables were even marginally significant. Specifically, the coefficient for the college graduate dummy was negative (indicating a greater propensity to choose correct answers) and significant at the .10 level in two of the regressions.

The coefficients for age were consistently positive and frequently significant.[36] This indicates that older respondents were more prone to choose incorrect answers. Gender proved significant in only one of the regressions. Males were more likely than females to select an inappropriate method for cooking the fish filet. Finally, the dummy variable for Sunrise Spread was always negative and highly significant in four of the five regressions, which indicates that these respondents were less likely to choose incorrect answers than were respondents assigned to a Sunflower Fields advertisement.

---

[34]   The product dummy was also interacted with the multi-value categorical variables for income, education, and age. No significant interactions were found.

[35]   The highest income level was significant at the .05 level in three of the five probit equations, and at the .10 level in one equation.

[36]   All of the age dummy coefficients were significant at the .05 level in two of the regressions. The dummy for the highest age category (50+) was significant in one regression, and the dummy for the second-highest age category (40-49) was significant in an additional regression.

V. Conclusions

The primary goal of our inquiry was to determine whether heart-health claims in print advertisements for fats and oils that are low in saturated fat or trans fat will convey to consumers that such products are heart healthy even when added to an existing diet. Consumers might form this perception if they infer incorrectly from such ads that the featured product is lower in calories and fat than brands that do not advertise a heart-health benefit. Alternatively, consumers might conclude that the product acts in the manner of a pharmaceutical to reduce the risk of heart disease despite its high caloric content.

The results of our study do not support either theory. For the questions that dealt directly with the relative or absolute caloric content of the tested products, the average responses of consumers assigned to the heart-health claim ad conditions did not differ statistically from the responses of consumers who saw only nutrient content claims (*e.g.*, "low in saturated fat," or "no trans fatty acids"). Nor did respondents in the health claim conditions believe with greater regularity that simply consuming the products would lower the risk of heart disease.

For Sunflower Fields cooking oil, the simple nutrient content claims also displayed little impact on consumer perceptions in these areas. In general, the mean responses to the relevant questions did not differ from the scores for the Tombstone Control ad, which contained no health or nutrient content claims. The nutrient content claim exhibited greater impact in the Sunrise Spread tests. In comparison to the Tombstone Control respondents, the nutrient content claim respondents rated Sunrise Spread as more appropriate for use in a diet to lose weight, and as lower in calories relative to butter.

Taken together, these findings provide no basis for restricting heart-health claims in advertising for products such as those tested in our study. The additional health information linking a product's nutrient content composition to a specific health benefit did not distort consumers' perception of the product's caloric content or the means by which the oil or spread could reduce the risk of heart disease. Further, although we did not test claims in labeling, our results do not provide support for FDA's current ban on heart-health claims for many fats and oils. These health claims apparently do not mislead consumers and they provide truthful information concerning the relationship between saturated fat or trans fat content and heart disease.

These conclusions not withstanding, our results also suggest that respondents as a whole did not understand that the advertised products were high in calories. This misperception was particularly evident for Sunflower Fields cooking oil, even for the respondents in the control group who were not exposed to any nutrient content claims or health claims. For example, most respondents believed that Sunflower Fields was somewhat lower or much lower in calories than butter, when in fact all cooking oils are higher in calories than butter. Respondents exhibited a better understanding of the caloric profile of vegetable spreads (at least those in stick form), but nonetheless viewed regular use of the product as an appropriate part of a diet to lose weight.

Our research also provides insight concerning the effectiveness of several approaches to improving consumer understanding of the caloric density of the tested products and the manner in which the products should be used to achieve a heart benefit. One clear result is that respondents did not interpret "substitution" and "simple" advertising claims differently for these products. For either a nutrient content or a health claim, framing the ad copy to suggest that consumers try the product *instead of* a less healthy fat or oil did not inform consumers that the advertised product can pose a heart-health risk if added to an existing diet. It should be noted, however, that respondents did distinguish between a dietary addition and a dietary substitution when asked directly about this issue. Respondents in all of the test conditions perceived the products as healthier for the heart when substituted for butter rather than when simply added to the diet.

The results also reveal that disclosing the number of calories per tablespoon of either the cooking oil or spread does not alter the perceived heart healthiness of the advertised product. Although, for Sunflower Fields, the disclosure helped respondents provide more accurate answers to the question that asked directly about the number of calories per serving, the responses to other questions indicate that respondents did not understand the practical significance of the calorie information.

The calorie disclosure also performed poorly in the Sunrise Spread treatments. Indeed, disclosing calories at times shifted perceptions in the wrong direction, improving respondents' opinion of the vegetable spread as a diet aid, and also increasing purchase interest. Consumers clearly do not regard 90-120 calories as a negative product attribute, even when the relevant serving size is only one tablespoon.

Firm conclusions on the efficacy of disclosing total fat per serving are difficult given that this remedy was not tested for any of the Sunflower Fields treatments. The fat disclosure performed unevenly in the Sunrise Spread questioning, and never had more than a modest impact on the results.

From a public policy standpoint, our results emphasize the need for increased consumer education concerning the high caloric density of products in the fats and oils food group, and the implications of this fact for daily dietary decisions and heart health. In particular, consumers need to understand that, on a per-tablespoon basis, cooking oils contain as many or more calories than any other food, including butter. Nutrient content and health claims in labeling and advertising can complement these educational efforts by identifying the specific types and brands of foods that have the healthiest fat profiles and that can contribute most to heart health as a dietary selection within the fats and oils food category.

The poor performance of the calorie disclosure in our tests indicates that public education must not be limited to informing consumers about the absolute number of calories in these products. Consumers must understand more generally that the regular addition of any food product with 90-120 calories per serving can contribute significantly to weight gain and associated health problems unless compensating adjustments are made elsewhere in the diet.

Appendix A
Sunrise Spread Main Questionnaire

ESCORT RESPONDENT INTO INTERVIEWING ROOM. SEAT RESPONDENT AT TABLE. IF RESPONDENT INDICATED EARLIER THAT S/HE WEARS GLASSES FOR READING, BE SURE THAT S/HE IS WEARING THEM.

Hello, my name is_____from Cunningham Research. As mentioned earlier, we are conducting a study today about advertising. I am going to show you an advertisement. Please read it carefully and let me know when you are finished.

GIVE RESPONDENT AD. WHEN RESPONDENT INDICATES THAT S/HE IS FINISHED LOOKING, TAKE BACK AD AND REMOVE FROM VIEW.

1. What was the name of the product that was advertised?

> 1 SUNRISE SPREAD, SUNRISE, SUN, SUNRISE MARGARINE
> 3 OTHER
> 9 DON'T KNOW, DON'T REMEMBER OR NOT SURE

Since people often read ads more than once, I would like you to look at the ad again. When you are done, I will take back the ad and then ask you some questions. There are no right or wrong answers to these questions. If you don't know an answer, that's o.k., just say "I don't know."

GIVE RESPONDENT AD. WHEN RESPONDENT INDICATES THAT S/HE IS FINISHED LOOKING, TAKE BACK AD AND REMOVE FROM VIEW.

2. Although you may have told me this before, what was the name of the product that was advertised?

> 1 SUNRISE SPREAD, SUNRISE, SUN, SUNRISE MARGARINE **CONTINUE)**
> 3 OTHER **(TERMINATE)**
> 9 DON'T KNOW, DON'T REMEMBER OR NOT SURE **(TERMINATE)**

3. What were the main ideas that the ad communicated to you? (RECORD VERBATIM.
PROBE UNTIL UNPRODUCTIVE WITH: Anything else?)

4a. Did the ad say or suggest anything about the amount of trans fatty acids in Sunrise Spread?

     1 YES **(Go to Q4b)**
     2 NO **(Go to Q5)**
     9 DON'T KNOW, NOT SURE OR DON'T REMEMBER **(Go to Q5)**

4b. What did the ad say or suggest about the amount of trans fatty acids in Sunrise Spread?
(RECORD VERBATIM. PROBE UNTIL UNPRODUCTIVE WITH: Anything else?)

5. Did the ad say or suggest anything to you about the amount of calcium in Sunrise Spread?

     1 YES
     2 NO
     9 DON'T KNOW, NOT SURE OR DON'T REMEMBER

6a. Did the ad say or suggest anything to you about whether Sunrise Spread is healthy for your
heart?

     1 YES **(GO TO Q6b)**
     2 NO **(GO TO Q7)**
     9 DON'T KNOW, NOT SURE OR DON'T REMEMBER **(GO TO Q7)**

6b. What did the ad say or suggest about Sunrise Spread being healthy for your heart?
(RECORD VERBATIM. PROBE UNTIL UNPRODUCTIVE WITH: Anything else?)

7. So far I have been asking you to answer questions based just on what the ad said or suggested. Now I would like you to answer the following questions based on what the ad said or suggested, or on anything else you may know or believe.

7a. Please answer the next question using this card. **(HAND RESPONDENT CARD A)**
Suppose you added Sunrise Spread to your regular diet without making any other changes in what you eat. For example, suppose that in the past you didn't use any spread or butter on your toast or sandwiches, but now you start using Sunrise Spread on them. Do you think that adding Sunrise Spread to your diet would be

          1 Extremely bad for the heart
          2 Bad for the heart
          3 Somewhat bad for the heart
          4 Neither bad nor good for the heart
          5 Somewhat good for the heart
          6 Good for the heart
          7 Extremely good for the heart

          (Note to programmer: answers are presented in this order for version 1, and presented in reverse order in version 2)

          RECORD LETTER SELECTED_____ **(GO TO Q7b)**
          9 DON'T KNOW, NOT SURE OR DON'T REMEMBER **(GO TO Q8a)**

7b You said **(READ RESPONSE TO 7a).** Why did you say that?

RECORD VERBATIM. PROBE UNTIL UNPRODUCTIVE WITH: Anything else?)

8a Now I am going to ask a question that I want you to answer using this card. **(HAND RESPONDENT CARD B)** Suppose you were to use Sunrise Spread instead of butter in cooking and on sandwiches. Do you think that using Sunrise Spread instead of butter would be

        1 Extremely bad for the heart
        2 Bad for the heart
        3 Somewhat bad for the heart
        4 Neither bad nor good for the heart
        5 Somewhat good for the heart
        6 Good for the heart
        7 Extremely good for the heart

(Note to programmer: answers are presented in this order for version 1, and presented in reverse order in version 2)

        RECORD LETTER SELECTED_____ **(GO TO Q8b)**
        9 DON'T KNOW, NOT SURE OR DON'T REMEMBER **(GO TO Q9)**

8b You said **(READ RESPONSE TO 8a)**. Why did you say that?

RECORD VERBATIM. PROBE UNTIL UNPRODUCTIVE WITH: Anything else?)

9a I would like you to use this card to answer the next question. **(HAND RESPONDENT CARD C)** Suppose someone you know has been using Sunrise Spread, and now decides to go on a diet to lose weight. Also suppose this person continues to use Sunrise Spread on a regular basis. Do you think that using Sunrise Spread on a regular basis would be:

        1 Extremely bad for losing weight
        2 Bad for losing weight
        3 Somewhat bad for losing weight
        4 Neither good nor bad for losing weight
        5 Somewhat good for losing weight
        6 Good for losing weight.
        7 Extremely good for losing weight

((Note to programmer: answers are presented in this order for version 1, and presented in reverse order in version 2)

9b You said **(READ RESPONSE TO 9a).** Why did you say that?

RECORD VERBATIM. PROBE UNTIL UNPRODUCTIVE WITH: Anything else?)

10 I would like you to answer the next question using this card.
(HAND RESPONDENT CARD D)
Suppose you are planning a meal and have three choices. Choice K is to bake a filet of fish with only lemon juice for liquid and seasoning. Choice L is to pan fry the fish with Sunrise Spread, and use only lemon juice as seasoning. Choice M is to pan fry the fish with butter, and use only lemon juice as seasoning.

(Note to programmer: the relevant sentence in version 2 would say: Choice K is to pan fry a filet of fish with butter, and use only lemon juice as seasoning. Choice L is to pan fry the fish with Sunrise Spread, and use only lemon juice as seasoning. Choice M is to bake the fish with only lemon juice for liquid and seasoning.)

10a Which method of cooking the fish do you think would be best for your heart? Would you say

K. Bake a filet of fish with only lemon juice
L. Pan fry the fish with Sunrise Spread & use only lemon juice as seasoning
M. Pan fry the fish with butter, and use only lemon juice as
   Seasoning

(Note to programmer: present answers in the order asked in the question above for Version 2)

(IF RESPONDENT GIVES MORE THAN ONE CHOICE, RECORD ALL NUMBERS GIVEN.)

RECORD NUMBER OR NUMBERS SELECTED_____
9 DON'T KNOW, NOT SURE OR DON'T REMEMBER

10b You said **(READ RESPONSE TO 10a).** Why did you say that?

RECORD VERBATIM. PROBE UNTIL UNPRODUCTIVE WITH: Anything else?)

10c Which of the remaining choices do you think would be better for your heart? (IF RESPONDENT GIVES MORE THAN ONE CHOICE, RECORD ALL NUMBERS GIVEN.)

        RECORD NUMBER OR NUMBERS SELECTED_____
        9 DON'T KNOW, NOT SURE OR DON'T REMEMBER

10d You said (**READ RESPONSE TO 10c).** Why did you say that?

RECORD VERBATIM. PROBE UNTIL UNPRODUCTIVE WITH: Anything else?)

11 I would like you to use this card to answer the next question. (**HAND RESPONDENT CARD E)** Based on what the ad says or suggests, or anything else you may know or believe, would you say that one tablespoon of Sunrise Spread is

        1 Much higher in calories than one tablespoon of butter
        2 Somewhat higher in calories than butter
        3 About equal in calories to butter
        4 Somewhat lower in calories than butter
        5 Much lower in calories than butter

(Note to programmer: answers are presented in this order for version 1, and presented in reverse order in version 2)

        RECORD LETTER SELECTED_____
        9 DON'T KNOW

12. I would like you to use this card to answer the next question. (**HAND RESPONDENT CARD F)** Based on what the ad says or suggests, or anything else you may know, about how many calories are in one tablespoon of Sunrise Spread? Would you say

        1 More than 200 calories
        2 151-200 calories
        3 101-150 calories
        4 51-100 calories
        5 0-50 calories

(Note to programmer: answers are presented in this order for version 1, and presented in reverse order in version 2)

RECORD LETTER SELECTED_____
9 DON'T KNOW

13. How interested would you be in buying the product?
(READ CHOICES AND CIRCLE ONE ANSWER)

    1 Not at all interested
    2 Not very interested
    3 Somewhat interested
    4 Very interested
    5 Extremely interested

14. Have you been on a diet to lose weight at any time during the last year?

    1 YES
    2 NO
    9 DON'T KNOW

(HAND RESPONDENT CARD G)
15. Which of the following describes your education?

    1 Some High School or less
    2 High School Graduate
    3 Some College or Technical School
    4 College Graduate
    5 Post Graduate
    9 Refused

(HAND RESPONDENT CARD H)
16. Which letter on this card best describes your household's total income before taxes in 2003?

    1 Under $25,000
    2 $25,000 to $49,999
    3 $50,000 to $74,999
    4 $75,000 or more
    9 Refused

That's all the questions I have for you. Thank you very much. Would you please sign this certification page so I can show my supervisor that I interviewed you? You may be contacted later to verify that the interview occurred, but information you provide will be kept confidential and will not be used to sell you anything.

RESPONDENT CERTIFICATION

I certify that I was shown a print ad, asked some questions about it, and paid $5.00 for my participation.

RESPONDENT NAME (PRINT)_____

SIGNATURE_____
DAYTIME PHONE_____
HOME PHONE, IF DIFFERENT_____
DATE_____

INTERVIEWER CERTIFICATION

I hereby certify that all of the above information was obtained by me from the respondent named above, who is not personally known to me. I agree to provide this affidavit under oath, immediately upon request.

INTERVIEWER NAME (PRINT)_____

SIGNATURE_____
DATE_____

Relationship Between Probability of Selecting Incorrect Response and Demographic Characteristics, Probit Coefficients (Conditional Mean Imputation Estimators)

	Adding to Diet (1)	Good for Losing Weight (2)	Cooking Method (3)	Calories Relative to Butter (4)	Number of Calories (5)
Income (Relative to Less Than $25,000)					
$25,000 - $49,999	-0.1507 (0.1244)	0.0170 (0.2077)	-0.1246 (0.1205)	-0.0350 (0.1220)	-0.1894 (0.1270)
$50,000 - $74,999	-0.2064 (0.1347)	-0.0325 (0.2320)	-0.1830 (0.1327)	-0.1376 (0.1334)	-0.2686 ** (0.1382)
$75,000 or above	-0.3597 ** (0.1504)	-0.1947 (0.2707)	-0.3799 ** (0.1553)	-0.2821 * (0.1529)	-0.4865 ** (0.1598)
Education (Relative to Some High School or Less)					
High School Graduate	0.0988 (0.2143)	0.0664 (0.3614)	0.2728 (0.2102)	0.2078 (0.2210)	-0.0559 (0.2256)
Some College or Technical School	0.0111 (0.2111)	-0.1272 (0.3575)	0.0425 (0.2086)	0.2732 (0.2199)	0.1470 (0.2233)
College Graduate	-0.1610 (0.2183)	-0.6364 * (0.3695)	-0.3935 * (0.2200)	0.0353 (0.2284)	-0.0559 (0.2322)
Post Graduate	-0.0021 (0.2440)	-0.1915 (0.4251)	-0.3864 (0.2515)	0.0173 (0.2565)	0.1678 (0.2603)
Age (Relative to 21 - 39)					
30 - 39	0.1543 (0.1124)	-0.0404 (0.1993)	0.1114 (0.1177)	0.1820 ** (0.1168)	0.3055 ** (0.1203)
40 - 49	0.3019 ** (0.1127)	0.2540 (0.2029)	0.3538 ** (0.1163)	0.3270 ** (0.1208)	0.3270 ** (0.1208)
Over 50	0.3058 ** (0.1142)	0.2366 (0.2061)	0.1041 (0.1192)	0.4455 ** (0.1181)	0.4460 ** (0.1234)

	Adding to Diet	Good for Losing Weight	Cooking Method	Calories Relative to Butter	Number of Calories
	(1)	(2)	(3)	(4)	(5)
Been on Diet to Lose Weight					
Yes	-0.0205 (0.0827)	0.1806 (0.1510)	0.0605 (0.0851)	0.0273 (0.0844)	-0.0415 (0.0867)
Gender					
Male	0.0720 (0.0932)	0.0048 (0.1644)	0.3765 ** (0.0930)	0.1210 (0.0938)	0.1186 (0.0978)
Tested Product					
Sunrise Spread	-0.2214 ** (0.0806)	N/A	0.0750 (0.0834)	-0.3282 ** (0.0835)	-0.2199 (0.0856)
Constant	0.4935	0.4297	0.5903	0.4499	-0.1878
Number of observations	1,086	345	1,086	999	929
Chi-square for Overall Significance	30.81	20.42	81.43	45.17	35.09

Note: Figures in parenthesis are standard errors. * $p < 0.10$, ** $p < 0.05$. (1) Probability of answering "Somewhat good," "Good," or "Extremely good" to: How good for the heart is adding product to diet? (2) Probability of answering "Somewhat good," "Good," or "Extremely good" to: How good for losing weight is regular use of product? (3) Probability of answering "Sauteeing with Sunflower Fields," "Sauteeing with Sunrise Spread," or "Sauteeing with butter" to: What is the most heart-healthy method for cooking a fish filet? (4) Probability of answering "Much lower in calories than butter" to: How does tested product compare in calories to butter? (5) Probability of answering "0-50 calories" to: How many calories are in a serving of the tested product?

www.ingramcontent.com/pod-product-compliance
Lightning Source LLC
Chambersburg PA
CBHW081219170526
45165CB00009B/2876